We acknowledge the traditional owners of the land on which this
book was written and made: the Wurundjeri and Bunurong people
of the Kulin nation, and the Gadigal and Cammeraygal people of
the Eora Nation. We pay respect to the custodians of these lands
on which grains were grown and milled and bread has been made,
and stories and recipes shared, for more than 60,000 years.

country loaf

Baker Bleu

Baker Bleu

bake it till you make it

Mike Russell
with Emma Breheny

murdoch books
Sydney | London

Contents

Foreword

By Neil Perry

I met Mike Russell in March 2009, at Rockpool Bar & Grill's opening in Sydney. He came to us as a young pastry chef – at that stage of his career, I had no idea he had a master-baker alter ego. He settled into the upstairs kitchen working alongside the group's executive pastry chef, Catherine Adams. More often than not he could be found rolling brioche buns and breads – he definitely was at home with them. Mike spent over nine months with us, and I admit I was a little disappointed when he resigned; I really liked him and he was a great part of the team. But given that he was leaving to follow his passion for baking and work in a proper bakery, my disappointment turned into hope that one day he could follow his dream and indeed be an accomplished baker.

I hadn't heard anything from him or, to be honest, thought about him again, until 2016. Ben Shewry invited me to Melbourne to cook a course as part of a fundraising dinner for Helping Hoops, a charity that worked with disadvantaged children. Mike had formed a great relationship with Ben and was providing the bread course for that dinner.

Well, when I tried the bread, I was immediately struck by its quality: perfect chewy crumb, dark crust and a long lingering lactic sour taste. This was truly magnificent bread; this bread moved me. I immediately asked Mike if he would consider supplying Rockpool Bar & Grill. He said it'd be impossible: he was stuck in a small bakery in Elsternwick that was at capacity. That was disappointing! I could understand, but I wasn't used to a 'no' from a supplier. He promised me that once they moved to a new bigger bakery in Caulfield, we would be on the list of new clients.

He made good on his word at the end of 2018. I was extremely happy. To me it was the best bread in Melbourne by far, in fact, I would go as far as to say you could put one of their bakeries in London, Paris or San Francisco, and it would stick out for its quality. To offer it at the temple of great produce, Rockpool Bar & Grill in Melbourne, was a no-brainer. We had the best fish and meat: why not the best bread? At that stage I guess Mike and I could have happily continued life as restaurant and supplier.

However, life had other ideas, including a global pandemic. What happened in 2020 is well-documented in the pages of history now. My response at the time was to start a charity, Hope Delivery, with the goal of feeding visa holders who had no support from the government. Later that year, I was chatting to a developer about a potential site that could house the charity and perhaps was big enough for some sort of social enterprise bakery. I wanted to give people the chance to buy a loaf of bread, and at the same time pay for another to be given to a family in need – an opportunity for people to pay it forward. Of course, I rang

> Well, when I tried the bread, I was immediately struck by its quality: perfect chewy crumb, dark crust and a long lingering lactic sour taste. This was truly magnificent bread; this bread moved me.

Mike to talk me through what a bakery might look like, and the costs associated with setting one up. By the end of our discussion over a period of several weeks, I had a good idea what was involved, and what the outlay would be.

Fast-forward to late 2020, at a meeting with Charles Mellick and Matthew Barakat, one of the partners and his leasing offsider at Pallas, the developers of the building where my new restaurant Margaret was being built. They had a new project right next door to Margaret, and they offered it to me. I guess I could have opened a restaurant – that's what they expected. But I wanted to do something that added amenity to the Double Bay area, something the community could use daily, so immediately I thought of Mike and Baker Bleu. This site was perfect for retail and food service, and facing north, it trapped the sun all day.

After a quick phone call, I convinced him to come and have a look. He arrived with his business partner and wife, Mia. I like to think she is the financial brains behind the operation, and Mike is the muscle – they are truly a dynamic duo. Well, at dinner that night at Rockpool Bar & Grill Sydney, I not only convinced them that Sydney needed their services, but I also established that they were, as a couple, really decent people who shared a like-minded vision with my family. A few days later we all agreed that my wife Samantha, Mike, Mia and I would partner to open a Baker Bleu bakery in Double Bay. Well, it wasn't as simple as that, but that's the gist of it.

And what a fabulous ride it has been, opening this jewel for the community that has, in turn, lapped it up. Amazing bread, pastries, sandwiches, pizza, coffee and drinks all in a beautiful space that offers take away or the option to dine on the street soaking up the sun.

Now they have written this extraordinary book, full of wise words and beautiful pictures. It not only explains the fundamentals of sourdough but demystifies it so that anyone can give it a go. It showcases the amazing breads and pastries that Baker Bleu is renowned for, but more than that,

it is also a view into the wonderful plethora of things that can be done with bread and pastry, how far you can take it, and how central it is to a great life.

If I have seen one thing over the past couple of years to convince me, it is how much people enjoy Baker Bleu and all the wonderful things it offers. So it stands to reason that this beautiful book will not only sit on people's bookcases but, more importantly, it will live in their kitchens, being thumbed through, and of course, cooked out of, often.

Introduction

How we got here

Most people see Baker Bleu as a much bigger, slicker business than it really is. They imagine lots of people behind us, with deep pockets who help make the day-to-day easier. Maybe it's because of the restaurants in Melbourne that serve our bread, or the beautiful details of the last two shops we opened.

I'm not downplaying any of that. I'm proud of what Baker Bleu is today. But the story of how we got here, baking forty thousand items each week and regularly selling out of things, is not the tale you might expect.

When my partner Mia and I first started Baker Bleu, it was just the two of us. Literally. I'd bake, Mia would serve, we'd clean everything down and do it again the next day. We were scrappy. We were new in town. We had our life savings, three bread recipes and nothing else. But we were hungry to do something of our own.

I had spent much of my 20s in search of that thing that made me tick. I was determined to avoid a log-on log-off, collect-a-paycheque job that seemed to be the common trajectory. I wanted to do something that lit me up.

Discovering baking when I was 25 was one of those corny moments you hear about where everything clicked. It was a fork in the road, taking me off an assembly line of jobs I couldn't care less about, and down a path of challenge, pride and fulfilment. I had found my thing.

I loved baking bread because it was making something from start to end. It was a craft that had been practised for centuries using the same basic elements: flour, water, heat, time. And yet every time you did it, you were back at square one, no matter how many years you'd been baking. A baker is only as good as their last loaf.

My new obsession grew into a vocation, with jobs in several top bakeries in Sydney and Melbourne. After trying many careers – from studying film-making to working in advertising, then acting – I felt like bread was going to stick. I pestered Mia night and day about opening our own bakery.

After about five years of this, she agreed. Our plan was to sell our apartment, move cities, Mia would juggle the business and working her nine-to-five job, and we'd just give it a go. We'd create the thing that had kept my mind alive with ideas during early mornings, late nights and weekends working for other people.

In December 2016, Baker Bleu was born. It was as basic as it gets. No employees. No backers. I remember walking out the back of our tiny bakery one day and calling Mia, saying, 'We're nuts. Every other bakery we know has at least three people behind it. What are we doing? We're fools.'

I want people who read this book to believe in themselves the way we did. I want you to trust that you can bake amazing bread at home (and maybe even turn it into a business, like we did).

> The way I see it today, how far we pushed ourselves to create something people love is proof that not all dreams are crazy. Normal people can do incredible things.

I don't want to make it hard for you. That's the difference between this book and other bread books. At Baker Bleu, we looked for all kinds of ways to make running a bakery easier. There's no shame in this. You should also take the easy road to delicious bread.

That's what this book is all about. Beautiful bread that's even more rewarding because of how simple it is to fit into your life. Once you make one of our core bread recipes – whether it's bagels or a classic country loaf – there are at least a couple of other things you can make from that same dough.

This is a book to be used, a lot. We hope it ends up splattered with dough, dusted in flour, splashed with tartine toppings, smeared with mustard from sandwiches and earmarked from front to back.

WHAT THIS BOOK GIVES YOU

- A 'real life' approach to making bread

- Multipurpose recipes: one recipe, many options

- Ways to upcycle your bread

- Ease, not technical details

- A window into running your own bakery

Who is Baker Bleu?

At the outset, I had none of the connections someone might need for a career in food, and neither did Mia. In fact when I started trying to get baking jobs, I was told I was too old to learn. I was 26.

My childhood in Sydney was very middle class, with a dad who had a job in upper-middle management and lived in constant trepidation of his job being 'restructured' or his role being made redundant.

Me, I lived in fear of that kind of existence. I knew I wanted to do something with my life that was about more than my next promotion. But when you're young, you stick to what you know. Everyone around me had been to university. I followed the same path, although I managed to convince my parents that art school was close enough.

> In my spare time, I was drawn to anything that involved process or craft. Working with my hands and using raw materials to create something that reflected the care I put into it really appealed to me.

After I finished a degree in media arts, the pressure was on to get a steady job. I spent two miserable years writing ads, then I knew it was time to trust my gut and pursue something with more soul.

I looked into making charcuterie, to the point of even contemplating pig farming. I explored the world of brewing cider. I did a year-long pastry course through a technical college. In the background, I worked a bunch of short-term jobs washing dishes, pulling beers at bars and waiting tables.

In my spare time, I was drawn to anything that involved process or craft. Working with my hands and using raw materials to create something that reflected the care I put into it really appealed to me.

Doing that pastry course in 2008, along with trips overseas where Mia and I ate dozens of tapas and pintxos, were both little bricks in the road that led me to bread.

Mia spent a year of her business degree studying in Barcelona, where she was exposed to a totally different way of thinking about food. I visited as much as I could from London, where I was working. Every trip got me thinking about the simplicity behind Spain's food culture.

Great bread was the vehicle for an array of simple combinations: manchego and serrano ham; anchovies and pickled chilli; tomatoes with nothing more than salt and olive oil. A visit to Argentina a few years later, where tapas culture is just as lively, got my brain ticking.

Mia says I get fixated on one thing: I polish my shoes a lot; we've always owned the same breed of dog. That type of personality suits bread-making. (It's also infuriating to live with.) Back home in Sydney, opening a pintxos bar became my obsession.

As the idea percolated, I started thinking about what bread I would serve the pintxos on, and decided I would bake it myself. That took me down a rabbit hole that only got deeper.

By this point, I'd gotten a job in the pastry section at one of Australia's best-known restaurants, Rockpool Bar & Grill, which was established by Neil Perry. Here, I learned how to make everything from brioche to cookies and cold desserts, but more and more, all I wanted to do was bake bread.

When I wasn't working, I'd bake at home from Jim Lahey's *The Sullivan Street Bakery Cookbook*. Following his 24-hour loaf recipe, I was blown away by the fact that such good results could come from such a simple method that could easily slot into your routine.

The next step was for me to get a proper baking job. I was turned down at lots of places because of my age, but finally, after begging them to hire me, I landed a job at the city outpost of Bourke Street Bakery, one of Sydney's earliest new-wave artisan bakeries, those places making good sourdough bread far superior to what we'd been eating before.

I didn't care about pay. As soon as I started, it felt like the perfect fit. Don't get me wrong: every aspect was a steep learning curve for someone who had virtually no professional training in breadmaking. All I'd done was bake a few dozen loaves at home.

Making sourdough bread or yeasted Italian doughs, hand-shaping and crafting croissants, and working at a much larger scale pushed me. But I also couldn't stop thinking and talking about bread. Just ask Mia.

Mia's story

7:30am in a bakery looks very different to the trading floor of a major bank. Standing in a flour-covered apron, rolling bagels or packing bread for delivery, I would think about how I had spent my mornings just a few months earlier, suited up, headset on, facing a wall of screens that tracked the financial markets.

From the outside, it probably seems like a tear in the fabric of your life, to change everything so radically. And to others around me, Baker Bleu definitely came as a shock. But running an artisan bakery was actually not an enormous leap for me.

Wholesome food and nutritious eating became a big part of my life in my late teens. I had grown up as a latch-key kid of migrant parents in the suburbs of Sydney. They had left the formerly communist Yugoslavia, where their childhoods were spent gathering snails after it rained for extra protein and picking wild asparagus to sell at the markets for extra money.

My parents overcompensated for their humble upbringings and created an Australian home of abundance and convenience. Instant noodles, Wonder White bread, chips, chocolate, sugary soft drink and cordial were pretty common in our cupboards. There was no chance my sister and I were going to go hungry, or miss out on any of the luxuries of Western life.

It's no wonder that by the time I was a teenager, I was paralysed with a serious case of irritable bowel syndrome and on the verge of developing a stomach ulcer.

Once I was old enough to take control of the situation, I explored the world of wholefoods and healthy eating. I gravitated to the bread that my parents would have grown up eating: rye or spelt loaves, made with sourdough starter. It didn't take long for me to feel like an energetic, vibrant person again.

By the time I was an adult in the early 2000s, more and more artisan bakeries opened in Sydney offering fresh sourdough. I thought what these bakeries were doing was absolutely amazing, especially because they were creating a market for something that was truly lacking. Not only was bread getting healthier but it tasted better, too.

I was very interested in food by this point, although I never envisioned I would run one of these bakeries myself.

Not knowing what career I wanted, I enrolled in the broadest degree I could: business, in a double degree with arts to keep it interesting. I was the first person in my family to go to university, which was a huge source of pride for my parents.

I leapt at the chance to study languages abroad for a year, choosing Barcelona. That began the second chapter of my food education.

Yes, I went to my classes, but I found my days revolved around food. I would go to the markets and bakeries each day, and discover new things. If I went to a new city in Spain or Europe, the first thing I would do was wander through the markets.

Mike was working in London at this time, so that we could be closer to each other, and whenever he came to visit me in Barcelona, we'd explore all the food the city had to offer.

Tapas really excited us. Because the plates were so simple, it all came down to the quality of the ingredients. We both realised that good bread was the basis of almost every tapa.

As Mike went further and further down the baking path, I could tell this wasn't a temporary obsession like other things he'd gotten into. He talked about bread all the time, and I mean: All. The. Time.

As we re-evaluated what we both wanted in our early 30s, we decided to give a bakery a go. I had my banking job as some security for us, and I trusted Mike's dedication and talent.

We knew we would open our first bakery in Melbourne for practical reasons but also because we loved the city's interest in food. It felt closer to what we'd enjoyed most about Europe.

But telling our families we were selling our Sydney apartment we'd saved so hard for to fund a bakery? Not everyone was thrilled.

> As we re-evaluated what we both wanted in our early 30s, we decided to give a bakery a go. I had my banking job as some security for us, and I trusted Mike's dedication and talent.

My risk-averse parents were particularly devastated that their university-educated daughter with a steady career was putting it all on the line to help her partner open a bakery. My dad was adamant that you should always work for somebody else. He was so upset he didn't speak to us for months. It felt like somebody had died.

Nine months after we moved to Melbourne, we felt we should call my parents to let them know we had signed a shop lease. The next day my dad, a former builder now in his 70s, eagerly got in the car and drove to Melbourne to help us set up the bakery on a shoestring budget.

Southern European families will drop everything if you need help. If you ask for something, it's not really a question; it's an instruction. The village mentality kicks in. Knowing they couldn't give us any money, my parents wanted to try and buffer us from the risks of business in another way. That ended up being with blood, sweat and tears.

Not only did my dad's building expertise come in handy, he also learned how to sew the hundreds of couche linen blankets we needed for the bread.

When we outgrew our first tiny bakery a couple of years later, he was back in Melbourne in a flash, working six days a week to help set up our much bigger operation. I will never forget the day the seven-tonne oven was craned into the bakery. The penny dropped for my dad: he was in awe of what he helped create. Our harshest critic became our biggest supporter. I really don't know how we would have done it without him.

I kept working my finance job after we opened the bakery, dropping down to part-time hours so I could help Mike on the days the bakery was open. Later I used some annual leave and long service leave to give us some financial stability.

In the early days, juggling both jobs, I was working almost non-stop. I'd be a shop assistant or delivery driver for the bakery half the week, go to the bank on the other days, and stay up each night doing admin for the business. When you're that busy working, it almost feels like part of your life has gone missing. At one point I was even suffering dizzy spells because I was racing around so much.

I wouldn't change much about the path I've chosen, but at the top of the list would be outsourcing things sooner. I had that common small-business-owner mentality that it's easier to do something yourself. But it takes a toll.

Finance taught me a lot of things that I could use in the new business: about structure, technology, money and how to navigate the corporate world. And I knew how to take on a sensible amount of debt. I think that's what's helped us transform a passion project into a serious business employing more than 80 people.

I think most people assumed I'd continue working at the bank for as long as we had the bakery because I'd need to support Mike. Four years after we opened Baker Bleu, though, I finally quit my steady job. It was a huge step, but it proved to all my friends and family that this business was not a hobby.

I never would have thought to start my own business, but the Croatian mentality I've inherited kicked in and I decided if Mike was going to do this, I'd be there with him all the way.

I'm so glad I did because throughout this journey, I've surprised myself with the reserves of energy and resilience that were hiding within me.

Mia Russell

How to build a bakery from scratch

In 2011, we ended up in Melbourne because Mia got transferred there by the bank she worked for.

For me, it meant finding another baking gig, and landing a job at Baker D. Chirico, one of the first bakeries in Australia to start baking sourdough, which gave me some of the best foundations in baking I could ask for.

Everything was done the right way. Each loaf was hand-shaped and we baked everything through the night, in shifts. I learned about the discipline of the mixing bowl. Knowing how to treat dough just by looking at it. How to be aware of temperature. What the dough needed to perform.

Daniel Chirico, the owner, also showed me how to maintain your workspace to a high standard. Sweeping was a religion; I reckon we had the cleanest floor of any bakery in Australia.

Every place I worked showed me something else that, all together, have made me the baker I am today. I think that's part of being in a hospitality community. We all learn from one another, add it to our own experiences, and create something of our own.

Returning to Sydney and working at Iggy's Down Under in Bronte, I saw a completely different workflow to that at Baker D. Chirico. Loaves were rested at cooler temperatures overnight for a very long, slow ferment. No bakers were working overnight to have everything baked and ready for the morning. Instead we baked hot and fast from 4am.

The bread that we pulled from the ovens was extremely dark on the outside, but with a milk-coloured interior that was nearly as smooth as butter. I knew that this was the style of bread I liked. I also saw this was the way to run a business. It was better for the baker, better for the bread.

I lived a five-minute walk from the bakery and could bake in the morning, finish work and go for a swim at the beach, five minutes in the other direction. Mia and I had saved enough to buy an apartment in this beachside suburb. It was a fantastic life.

But I still wasn't completely satisfied. I wanted to create my own bakery. A business, yes, but something for Mia and I to call our own and be proud of. It was about seeking something genuine and honest, rather than building an empire.

We loved Melbourne when we lived there the first time and, being a smaller and cheaper city to live in than Sydney, we thought it was a better place to start a business.

Mia asked for a transfer in her bank job and back to Melbourne we went. We had a chorus of family and friends telling us we were crazy, that we'd be back soon, that we were too old to start a bakery.

On the day we sold our apartment to fund the business, someone we knew even told us: 'Mark this day, because I'm telling you, you're making the biggest mistake of your life.'

When we got to Melbourne, I got a job driving deliveries for a boutique wine store. It was a great way to get to know the city better and suss out which neighbourhood we should open our bakery in.

A lease eventually came up in a stretch of shops in Melbourne's south, on a sleepy part of a main road in Elsternwick, near the city's Jewish neighbourhoods. It wasn't a hip part of town, but it had the fundamentals we thought a successful bakery needed: families living nearby, on-street parking, and the space needed very few changes.

We got ourselves set up and opened the doors in December 2016. We knew we would trade three days a week at first and only sell three things: bagels, baguettes and a two-kilogram country loaf. But a name was much harder to decide on. Most people use their own name for bakeries but, given mine was hardly memorable, I started playing around with a childhood nickname I was given due to my red hair: Blue. Incongruous nicknames are a strange Australian tradition that makes no sense, but I figured that taking that and spelling it the French way summed up who I was: an Aussie baker using French techniques. Baker Bleu was the perfect fit.

When we opened, Mia worked four days at the bank, then spent the rest of the week getting ready for our manic weekends of trade. She'd serve customers, shape bagels and keep things organised. She's the stabiliser in the business.

Officially in business

Initially, people didn't know what to make of us. Three products, three days a week, no sign, no coffee, no croissants? But we loved how focused we were on doing one thing and doing it really well.

On our first day, we made $300 and I remember Mia thinking, 'Wow!'. After all the tough talk from our friends and families, our expectations were clearly pretty low.

Word gradually spread about our ultra-chewy dark loaves and, eventually, long queues would form along our otherwise-quiet stretch of Glen Eira Road.

Before that, though, we'd often give loaves away to friends and people I knew from my time working at Baker D. Chirico. Eventually, through one of these channels, word of our bread made its way to influential Melbourne chef Andrew McConnell, who has half-a-dozen restaurants.

He came to the bakery to check it out for himself. Of course, when he arrived, I was hauling 10-kilo bags of salt off the pavement and was covered in sweat. In the end, it didn't matter. He loved the bread and asked us to create something for his restaurant Cutler & Co. I broke one of my golden rules about never doing custom orders and signed our first (and now largest) wholesale customer.

The bakery rises

This was when things really started to take off. We were only six months old and realised we needed a delivery van. We thought that would happen years down the track.

When you start a business, people tell you that you'll be doing long hours. They might pass you their accountant's number or put you in touch with a good plumber. But no one prepares you for the exhaustion you feel deep in your bones, day after day after day.

Mia had to go on long service leave to keep up with managing our wholesale orders, which had now grown from just Andrew's restaurant. The cat was out of the bag. Meanwhile, we were still baking out of a 60-square-metre shop with one four-deck oven.

It was time to find somewhere bigger to bake and – crunch time – our lease was nearly up. We'd been looking for a long time with no luck when a customer, who was a real estate agent, told us he'd help us. He really wanted us to stay in the area.

He found an enormous office building 10 minutes away, but it wasn't for lease. After a few meetings with the landlord, though, who saw a bakery as extremely risky, we miraculously got the keys. And then freaked out.

'It's so much money! It's perfect but it's too big for us. We'll never fill it!'

It was nearly six times bigger than our original bakery and we needed $2 million of equipment to be able to bake at the volumes we wanted.

And guess what? Now it's too small, even with our other Melbourne bakery that just does pastries and viennoiserie.

Thinking about where we started compared with where we are today, I pinch myself all the time. To now have opened a bakery back in our home town of Sydney, in partnership with one of Australia's culinary godfathers in Neil Perry, right next to his restaurant Margaret in Double

Bay, is honestly quite surreal. (And it's pretty fun to be able to say 'I told you so' to some of the people who doubted us.)

But most of all, I'm glad that Mia and I, two ordinary people, decided to step outside the tried-and-tested path and do something we believed in.

We're only talking about bread, one of the world's most common foods, but we're also talking about a staple food with thousands of years of history, and so many things have to go right to execute the perfect loaf.

That's why it feels so amazing sending people home with a brown paper bag that contains something you've spent hours nurturing.

That's the magic of baking.

THE BUILDING BLOCKS OF BAKING

I heard somewhere that bakers are happy people. It's a hard job but it produces a result, in bread, that feeds people one of the most fundamental foods of all. And if it's done well, it can make people smile.

What I love about bread is that it appears very simple – it's just flour, water and salt – but each time you make it, it's never quite the same.

The temperature will be different. The humidity might be higher or lower. The grain you use will vary. As a baker, you need to pay attention to all of that and listen to the dough. That forces you to be present, to slow down, to concentrate on the task in front of you.

For me, it was a humbling thing to discover.

Everything is about the dough

The dough dictates what you need
to do next. 'I've proofed enough,'
it says. 'I'm ready to be shaped.
I'm too cold, I'm not ready to
bake.' You don't say to the dough,
'Now we're going to bake you.'
It's telling you. It's dictating
to you. Once you accept that, you
will become a much better baker.

Baking bread requires attention to detail and nurturing. Not attention to detail and the task at hand like a pâtissier, but attention to detail even while you are not in front of what you're making. Particularly sourdough.

A good baker is always thinking about the complete process. I would go home after work and in the back of my mind, I'd be thinking: I hope the loaves are proving properly. I hope the warm night isn't affecting them. This was even the case when I was working for other people. So when we opened our own bakery, you can imagine how fixated I was.

Getting your head around sourdough can be tricky at first. You're looking after something alive, like a pet or farm animals. Are they warm? Are they hungry? When was the last time they were fed? Have they been out too long?

But sourdough is worth it. If you produce something made with yeast, it's not going to give you the same eating quality, the same digestive and nutritional benefits, or the same shelf life.

There are many ways to make leavened bread, but the fermentation process is really rewarding. If you're willing to make bread at home, creating and nurturing a starter is just another little part of that journey.

Our approach to bread

I'm not scientific, so a lot of people assumed baking would be a challenge for me. But through repetition, my knowledge has grown, and I'm now guided by instinct and process. By baking more and more, you too will familiarise yourself with what looks and smells right.

Bread-baking demands all the senses. Instead of taking a technical approach, I have relied on touch and feel, instinct and intuition. I encourage you to do the same.

Mia and I both love a dark crust on a loaf. Historically, bread was dark and chewy, so we bake ours the same way. But some customers will point at a Baker Bleu loaf and say, 'I don't want the burnt one.'

Bread is personal. You will figure out what you like and how long to bake your loaves. That's part of you developing your instincts and your knowledge of what the dough needs.

When I started baking, at first I was obsessed with learning how to shape perfectly. Then the next day, I'd be thinking about the loaf and scoring it and getting that amazing spring in the oven. Then I'd want the whole deck of loaves to have an amazing, even, dark colour. It's not that I was worried about whether each loaf would sell. It was a pride thing.

A large part of baking is about self-satisfaction. Think about all the steps involved. You'll cultivate a natural starter from scratch at home. You time its activity to perfect ripeness. You've sourced beautiful fresh flour and filtered water. The temperature of the room and mixing are just right. You rest overnight, the loaf is proofed to perfection and you are looking good to bake.

Now you have to execute a seamless transfer, score the loaf properly and then transfer again to the hot oven. The heat hits the loaf and it springs. A great crust is achieved then the deep colour comes later. It's almost a state of Zen.

Do you see why bakers are so happy now?

Getting started: the baker's toolkit

The main point I'll make about equipment is to avoid waste. You don't need to go out and buy brand-new appliances or a whole kit of things you'll never use again in your kitchen. I want you to adapt common kitchen tools and make the breadmaking work for you. You'll find any extra specialty tools listed in recipes.

Baking paper
You can re-use the same sheet of baking paper for multiple bakes.

Baking sheets or rectangular baking trays
These are essential for proofing and baking individual items like bread rolls, cookies, croissants, even our ciabatta loaves – the list goes on. Buy as many as you have room for.

Breadknife
How else will you enjoy all that bread?

Calculator
This will allow you to get your bakers' percentages correct for each recipe.

Cast-iron Dutch oven or casserole, with lid
This is like an oven within your oven. It's probably the most expensive piece of kit you'll need, but it's critical to mimic a proper bakery oven. It holds heat well, plus the lid traps steam. Choose a lid with a metal handle, not plastic. The bonus is it

will end up as the heartbeat of your kitchen: use it for ragù, ratatouille, poaching fruit and more.

Confoil tins
These small aluminium tins are normally used to make individual tarts and pies, of the kind you'd buy from your school tuckshop. We use them to make croissants and Danishes. Look for 11.5 cm (4½ inch) diameter tins and buy 16 if you want to make the recipes in this book.

Cookie cutters
Good for cutting your bread into the shapes you need for our tapas.

Dough scrapers (or pastry cards)
A dough scraper is the smallest part of your kit but will soon be your best friend. Use it to scrape down your bowls, your hands and keep all that dough in one place. You can find them at kitchenware shops or online. Don't spend more than $5 on a pastry card, and between $25–$40 on a metal dough scraper.

Dusting mix
This is the magic dust that will stop your loaf from sticking to benchtops, tea towels and other surfaces. Some people like semolina, others prefer rice flour, but my default is baker's flour. I won't list it in recipes, but you will definitely need this in your pantry.

Gastronorm pan
These are good for baking focaccia. We suggest two different sizes in the recipe, depending on whether you want to make one large focaccia or two small (see page 61).

Heatproof mats
These are great for putting hot things on, like preheated oven trays and Dutch ovens. But you can probably survive with things you already have in your kitchen, like chopping boards.

Kitchen scales
Everything in baking is measured by weight and volume, rather than cups. Find digital kitchen scales that are accurate and battery-operated and make sure they measure by the gram.

Loaf tins
Dark rye: 13 x 24 cm (5 x 9½ inch)

Challah tin (large): 33 x 10 x 10 cm (13 x 4 x 4 inch)

Challah tin (small): 22 x 10 x 10 cm (8½ x 4 x 4 inch)

Brioche: 22.5 x 14 x 9 cm (8½ x 5½ x 3½ inch)

Nordic Ware proofing tray with lid
An alternative to using baking sheets and tea towels, this is a really neat way to proof your bread items. You just pop the lid on and it's ready to go into your fridge for a nice slow ferment. If you'll be baking a lot, it's worth investing in one (or a couple!).

Oven mitts
Hauling a screaming-hot cast-iron pot in and out of the oven should not be done without some good oven mitts. Non-negotiable.

Pastry brush
You'll use this to apply glazes, eggwash, water to seal the edges of pastry, and so on.

Pie tin (aluminium or cast iron)
If you are a pie fan, you'll want one of these in your kit to enjoy our two sweet pies in the book.

Pizza stone or terracotta tile
Absolutely essential to get the right texture on your at-home pizza.

Plastic container with lid, 2 litres (4 cups)
This is good for resting doughs such as the ciabatta and bagel dough. If the old containers you're planning to use for your starter won't hold 2 litres, you'll need to find another that will.

Plastic tubs (large ones) with lids, upcycled yoghurt tubs, or similar
Sourdough starter requires tubs that can be sealed. I tend to rotate between two vessels of roughly the same size because you'll need to store your starter somewhere when you wash the other tub. So start collecting those old containers!

Ricotta baskets
You know those fancy cloth-lined bread baskets you see on Instagram and in bakeries? This is your version, except it's cheaper and more versatile. Find these at kitchenware shops.

Rolling pin
A must-buy item for making croissant dough, also helpful for several of the savoury recipes in the book. But you can always use an empty wine bottle.

Ruler or tape measure
This will be critical if you decide to tackle our croissant dough.

Everything about croissants involves precise layering, so measuring your pastry will be quite important.

Scoring tools
You can be as technical or lo-fi as you like here. A small serrated knife can do the job. If you shave with an old-fashioned razor, use one of those blades. Other scoring tools include a baking lame (if you want to go crazy; cost is approximately $20) or razor blades, which you can get from a shaving shop. We use Personna blades at Baker Bleu.

Stainless-steel bowl, 30 cm (12 inch) diameter
Your best friend throughout the process is the stainless-steel bowl. This is your mixer! More on this later.

Stainless-steel round pizza tray, 32 cm (12½ inches) diameter (or slightly larger than the base of your mixing bowl)
This is your lid to the dough-mixing bowl and is essential for pizza.

Stand mixer
An important piece of equipment if you want to make sweet pastries. It's expensive, yes, but I'm guessing that if you're someone keen to make croissant dough at home, you're already a keen baker and either own one or will get a lot of use out of it.

Tea towels
You'll need these to line and cover your ricotta basket when you're resting your loaf overnight.

Thermometer
This is essential for you to control your water temperature when feeding the starter. You'll spend about $40 on a probe thermometer (and you'll use it for far more than just baking).

Whisk
Needed for making many savoury and sweet creams.

Wire cooling rack
If you're a baker, you probably already have at least one of these. If not, they are easy to come by. Don't spend too much money.

Wooden pizza peel
Don't try and transfer your pizza from bench to oven without one, or you may end up regretting it.

Thinking Like A Baker

Room temperature

This part of the puzzle is an important one for the home baker. Where you keep your starter and your dough will be the key to your success. The dough is trying to grow and rise, and for that it needs a certain temperature. You don't dictate what happens to the dough, the dough dictates to you.

The place you keep your starter and dough should have a stable temperature. If you keep your dough in a spot with a different temperature the next time you bake, you can be pretty sure you'll end up with a different result. For example, the kitchen table might feel like the place, but it's a spot that can be super warm while the oven's on, then super cold when there's no one in the kitchen. You need to find an area where the temperature is consistent throughout a 24-hour cycle so you have reliable fermentation control.

This could be somewhere up high in a cupboard. Or somewhere lower down, but not on a bottom shelf and not on the floor. A general rule is to store your starter at least 900 millimetres (35½ inches) above the floor. Try a few spots and see what works.

When it comes to resting the dough, clear out your crisper drawer; this is the best spot for an overnight rest.

Water

A large percentage of your loaf is water. It's just as important as the grain. Therefore, it's essential that you filter your water.

You don't want any of the additional chemicals and metals that are found in tap water, such as fluoride, chlorine or aluminium, affecting your dough. All of these impede the fermentation process, particularly when you're building a natural starter. Not to mention the effect they have on your dough's flavour profile!

During the starter-building process, you are cultivating the organisms that are in the flour, the room, on your hands and in the water. The last thing you want to do is use water that has chemicals in it.

If you don't have a filter, boil the kettle and let it cool down to approximately 28°C (82°F) to get good results.

Flour

When it comes to flour, it's important to source the best quality you can.

Here in Australia, we're lucky to have a wide range of beautiful grain that's grown and then milled by skilled craftspeople. At Baker Bleu we source our grain from Wholegrain Milling Co. based in Gunnedah, NSW.

You will have access to different flour wherever you are in the world. The main thing to remember when selecting a flour is to get something that's local and that has at least 13 per cent protein content, which will help with gluten development.

The range that is available now, even in major supermarkets, is far better than it was. But I will say to read the label carefully, find out where it's from, check the protein content. Using good flour versus mass-produced, stale, industrial stuff could be the difference between your starter working or not.

Tips on flour suppliers are on page 232.

Reading recipes

Many of the recipes in this book look a little different to what you might be used to. The ingredients are listed not only with their weight or volume, but also with a percentage.

This is called a baker's percentage, and helps us easily scale recipes up (or down). When you're first starting to make bread, it can also help you get your head around what kind of dough you're working with: how wet or dry or stiff or active it might be.

Despite it looking precise, there's a bit of creative licence that goes into the maths. We're bakers, after all!

Here's how we calculate percentages:

Think of the ingredients as divided into two groups: flour, then everything else.

No matter what, the flour (or flours, if there's a mix) will always total 100%. This is what you're measuring the rest of the ingredients against, which are then presented as a ratio of the flour.

In the ingredients list below, for example, there are two types of flour. To work out their percentages, we add the two weights together, then divide each flour's weight by that total. That ensures that together our flours add up to 100%. In this case, it's 80% baker's flour, 20% wholemeal.

Our next-biggest ingredient is the water. To work out its ratio, we divide 450 grams (the weight of the water) by 600 grams (the combined weight of the flours), which gives us 0.75, or 75% of the weight of the flour.

Then it's the ripe starter: 180 grams divided by 600 grams gives us 30%.

We go down the list by weight and use the same formula to figure out the percentage for each, always dividing the ingredient's weight by the total flour weight, then multiplying by 100.

Country loaf:

Ripe starter	180 g (6½ oz)	30%
Strong (baker's) flour	480 g (1 lb 1 oz)	80%
Wholemeal stoneground emmer or spelt flour	120 g (4¼ oz)	20%
Filtered water	450 g (1 lb)	75%
Malt syrup	6 g (⅛ oz)	1%
Fine pink salt	16 g (½ oz)	2.7%

At a glance, you can tell this dough has a moderately high hydration (75%), but not as high as some doughs (you might see some at 85% or even 90%).

If you want to scale this recipe up by a quarter, say to get slightly bigger loaves, it's easy. As long as all of the ingredients still have the same ratio to one another, you know it will work.

The Recipes

MAKING A STARTER

In the book we use a sourdough starter that you will build and nurture yourself (see page 36).

When you are making a starter, it's like a puppy that you have to keep an eye on. Stick to the intervals for feeding, as it needs to be strong and healthy to make all these recipes sing.

That said, I encourage you to make bread fit into your groove. By that, I mean have a feeding schedule that fits into your life. I'm guessing that if you bought this book and have read this far then you are interested in food, but you're probably not a restaurant-going influencer type. You actually cook.

If you cook often, I suggest you feed the starter and make your bread around the time you cook dinner (or whatever time of day you're most in the kitchen).

What is a starter?

We'll be making a sourdough starter, and then using that to create a levain, which is the thing that will help your bread rise.

A lot of people tend to use the term levain interchangeably with sourdough starter, but they actually refer to different things.

Sourdough starter is the first step to get towards a levain, and, eventually, baking bread. A starter is simply flour and water that has taken on the cultures that naturally exist in the air and on our bodies, and fermented them. It's far removed from commercial yeast.

Starters give more flavour and aroma to baked goods thanks to all the wild bacteria and all the fermentation activity that happens in that humble vessel you've nurtured in your kitchen.

Levain takes some of this ripe starter and mixes it with fresh flour and water. This is what gets added to your bread dough, and you use it once for whatever it is you're baking. Your sourdough starter, on the other hand, is something you maintain and keep alive so it's there when you next want to bake.

A basic starter

Begin making your starter for the first time about five to seven days before you want to bake. Five days is the soonest that your starter will be ready; seven days gives you a safety net in case the starter isn't ripe enough.

The quantity this recipe makes is not an exact quantity that is going to be used when you start baking. It's more of a building block to get you on the road to a healthy, ripe starter that you can dip into when you are ready to bake.

The quantity is also in the sweet spot of being not uncomfortably huge, but large enough for the starter to generate its own bulk heat. This is important because if the quantity is too small, it will never get any fermentation heat going and you'll be on the back foot before you even begin baking.

Once you've got a healthy starter going, you can keep it on hand for your baking needs pretty much indefinitely.

DAY 1

BAKING INGREDIENTS AND PERCENTAGES		
Whole rye flour	300 g (10½ oz)	100%
Filtered water, at 28°C (82°F)	375 g (13 oz)	125%

On day 1, you are making your 'seed feed'. Half of this seed feed will be used in the day 2 feed.

Add the flour and water to the plastic or glass container you've selected to be the home for your starter (see baker's toolkit, page 28).

It's super important to use just your hands and your pastry card scraper to mix your starter: your fingers and nails carry lots of wild yeasts to activate the starter. Mix with one hand, starting just with your fingertips, working in a circular motion to create a slurry. This slurry quickly becomes a really wet dough that you mix through using your fingers. It should not require you to mix with your whole hand.

Make sure there are no dry bits on the outside of the container by using your pastry card to scrape down the sides of the container. Once you're done, you're looking for a smooth dough-like mix that resembles cooked porridge, with no dry bits or clumpy pieces of flour.

Cover the container with a clean cloth or tea towel and fasten it to the bowl with an elastic band. Stand the container for 24 hours in an area of the house where it's a stable, consistent temperature. The optimal temperature is 20°C (68°F). Don't leave your starter in an area less than 10°C (50°F).

DAY 2

BAKING INGREDIENTS AND PERCENTAGES		
Day 1 mix	200 g (7 oz)	111%
Whole rye flour	90 g (3¼ oz)	50%
Plain (all-purpose) flour	90 g (3¼ oz)	50%
Filtered water, at 28°C (82°F)	225 g (8 oz)	125%

Discard 475 g (1 lb 1 oz) day 1 mixture, leaving 200 g (7 oz) in the container, then add the flours and water to the same container and repeat the mixing process. It's important to use the same container you used on day 1; don't clean it or use a new one or you'll just throw away the microflora that is beginning to grow and form the basis of your healthy starter. This is such an important part of the process during which you're building the blocks of the sourdough culture.

When all ingredients are combined, stand for 12 hours in the same spot as before.

DAYS 3, 4 & 5

BAKING INGREDIENTS AND PERCENTAGES		
Starter from previous day	90 g (3¼ oz)	30%
Plain (all-purpose) flour	300 g (10½ oz)	100%
Filtered water, at 28°C (82°F)	270 g (9½ oz)	90%

Each day, discard the extra starter (or use it in something like the sourdough cookies on page 175), then repeat the mixing process with the same container and let it stand for 12 hours, as before. By days 3, 4 and 5, the starter should start to show bubbles 6–12 hours after mixing. You're looking for small-to-medium bubbles on the surface. Its aroma should be like a combination of strong yoghurt and bananas, and it shouldn't smell too alcoholic.

WHEN IS YOUR STARTER READY?

When it's ready, the starter should have medium-to-small bubbles on top, with an aerated appearance (but it shouldn't look too gassy). It should also be in the window of being ripe (approximately 6–12 hours after you mixed it). Look for the smells described above. Finally, taste it: the first flavour should be sweet and banana-bready, followed by a tangy aftertaste. If it's acidic all the way through and there's no sweetness at all, your starter is overripe.

The float test is the best way to make sure your starter is in the right window. Take a small spoonful of starter and drop it into a clear glass or measuring jug of water. If it floats to the top, or even partially floats, it's ready to bake with. If it's not ready, you can always leave it for another hour to ripen. If it's overripe, it will feel runny. Feed it again and wait 6 hours, again leaving it in an ambient environment. Either way, if your starter's not in the right state, your loaf just isn't going to perform, so it's not worth pushing ahead. Wait, and get a better result.

This is now your healthy, active starter, something you can keep alive for weeks, months, years or generations. Make it your baby.

→

DAY 1   DAY 2   DAY 3

DAY 4   DAY 5   DAY 6

MAINTAINING A STARTER

BAKING INGREDIENTS AND PERCENTAGES		
Starter from previous day	30 g (1 oz)	30%
Plain (all-purpose) flour	100 g (3½ oz)	100%
Filtered water, at 28°C (82°F)	90 g (3¼ oz)	90%

If you're baking regularly, you can continue to feed your starter daily using the quantities above. If, however, you're not baking regularly, store your starter in the fridge and feed it once a week; I hate seeing people waste flour and water by feeding a starter too often. Once a week is enough, trust me.

When you want to bake, remove your starter from the fridge and feed it twice at 12-hour intervals the day before you'll begin the recipe.

THE BREAD TIMELINE

To know when to start working on your bread, work backwards from when you want a finished loaf. Keep in mind that each phase has a window. Below are the two extremes in terms of timing. The slower pace may not suit your schedule, but you can adapt the timing of the cold fermentation method to suit you. Keep in mind that between these two extremes there's also a sweet spot with 15 hours of cold fermentation, which can be a kind of happy medium.

Quickest

FRIDAY	7am–9am feed your starter	~ 6 hours before starter is ripe
	1pm–3pm mix dough (1 hour)	~ 3 hours bulk rest
	5pm–7pm loaf goes into fridge	~ 12 hours fermentation
SATURDAY	5am–7am remove loaf from fridge	~ 3 hours proofing at room temperature
	8am–10am put loaf in oven	~ 1 hour bake plus 30 minutes cooling

Slowest

FRIDAY	5am–7am feed your starter	~ 12 hours before starter is ripe
	5pm–7pm mix dough (1 hour)	~ 3 hours bulk rest
	9pm–11pm loaf goes into fridge	~ 18 hours fermentation
SATURDAY	2pm–4pm remove loaf from fridge	~ 3 hours proofing at room temperature
	5pm–7pm put loaf in oven	~ 1 hour bake plus 30 minutes cooling

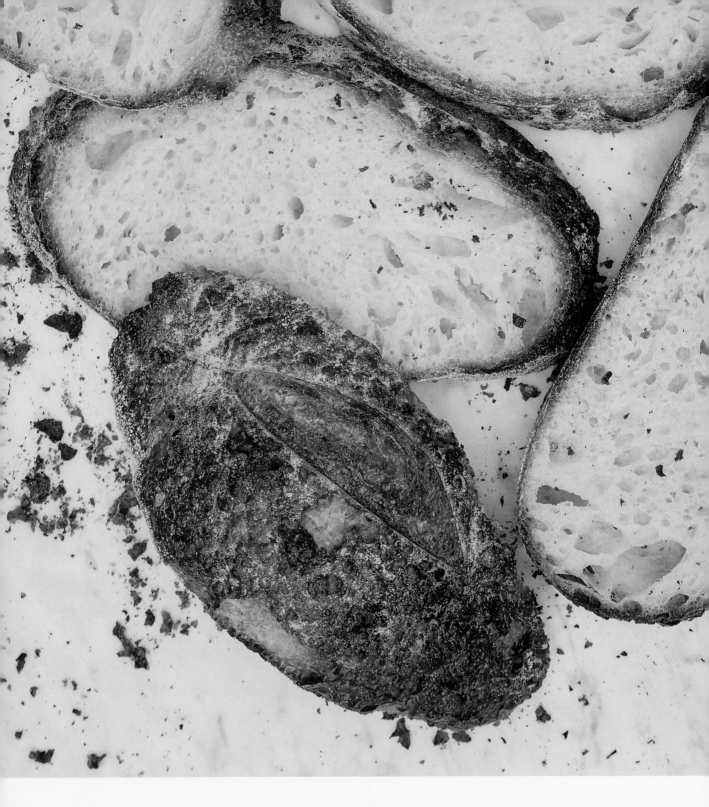

Country Loaf

→ Olive and walnut loaf → Rye-caraway loaf → Seeded spelt
loaf → Deep-dish focaccia → Olive fougasse

42–67

COUNTRY LOAF:
THE BEGINNING AND SOME ENDS

Once we got the lease on our first shop and spent lots of money on equipment, the pressure was on to make some bread. Good bread, at that. Much like a home baker just starting out, our own repertoire started with one loaf: the country loaf.

Everyone loves a country loaf. It's versatile, it's simple, it doesn't require any tricky shaping or added ingredients. At it's core, it's a traditional, naturally leavened loaf, made in a rustic French style with time-honoured techniques. The paths are endless, too: use fresh slices in sandwiches, tapas, tartines; or turn leftovers into toast, crackers, croutons or breadcrumbs.

Baker Bleu was built from the simple country loaf, with one style branching into many, and then other items added on top and around it. You can start your own baking journey with this recipe, too, since this basic dough can be flavoured easily, or turned into something else entirely, such as focaccia or fougasse. In fact, this chapter shows you exactly that.

A few tips before you start

- Feed your starter (see page 36) ahead of time. If your starter is kept at ambient temperature, feed it 6–12 hours before beginning this recipe. If it's been dormant in your fridge (i.e. you only feed it once a week), allow time for two feeds (so 12–24 hours).

- Weigh out your ingredients before you begin mixing. Things get messy.

- Always start by measuring the wet ingredients into the bowl first, in case you get any of the quantities wrong. It's easier to start again before you add the dry ingredients, after which you risk losing a whole batch of dough.

- Don't blindly follow the recipe, instead use your senses. The recipe really is just about the measurements and the mixing of the dough. After that, you need to look at and listen to the dough to figure out what it needs.

- Don't panic: if anything goes wrong, you can always make focaccia (page 61).

Don't panic: if anything goes wrong, you can always make focaccia.

→

Country loaf

MAKES A 1.2 KG (2 LB 12 OZ) LOAF

A rustic loaf with a flavourful, developed crust packing plenty of texture and crunch, and a complex, unctuous crumb on the inside.

This dough is also the starting point for the other recipes in this chapter – olive and walnut loaf, rye-caraway loaf, seeded spelt bread, focaccia and fougasse – while the cherry-chocolate bread follows much the same method.

BAKING INGREDIENTS AND PERCENTAGES		
Ripe starter (page 36)	180 g (6½ oz)	30%
Strong (baker's) flour	480 g (1 lb 1 oz)	80%
Wholemeal stoneground emmer or spelt flour	120 g (4¼ oz)	20%
Filtered water, at 28°C (82°F)	450 g (1 lb)	75%
Barley (or rice) malt syrup	6 g (⅛ oz)	1%
Fine pink salt	16 g (½ oz)	2.7%

PREPARING YOUR STARTER

1. Feed your starter 6–12 hours before you want to start mixing your dough. If you keep your starter in the fridge give it two feeds (see page 44), then pull it out an hour before you want to bake so it comes up to room temperature.

2. Do a float test (page 37) to check the starter is ready to bake with.

3. Once you've taken out the quantity you need for this recipe, do a standard feed of your bulk starter as noted on page 40 to keep it nice and healthy.

MIXING

1. Weigh out all remaining ingredients into separate bowls or containers as if you're running a professional operation. This is important in making sure you haven't forgotten anything. It also means everything is ready to go once you start getting your hands dirty.

2. Check the temperature of the water with your thermometer. You'll want it to be right on 28°C (82°F); anything colder will affect the timings. Add the water to your mixing bowl, followed by the starter – scoop this out with your hand; all the microbes from your skin will help to encourage your starter to grow. If it's perfectly ripe and ready, it will float like a cloud.

3. Add the malt syrup (image 01), then place both flours in the bowl (image 02). Finally, add the salt (image 03), checking it doesn't come into direct contact with the starter. Pause, and visually check off that everything is in the bowl.

→

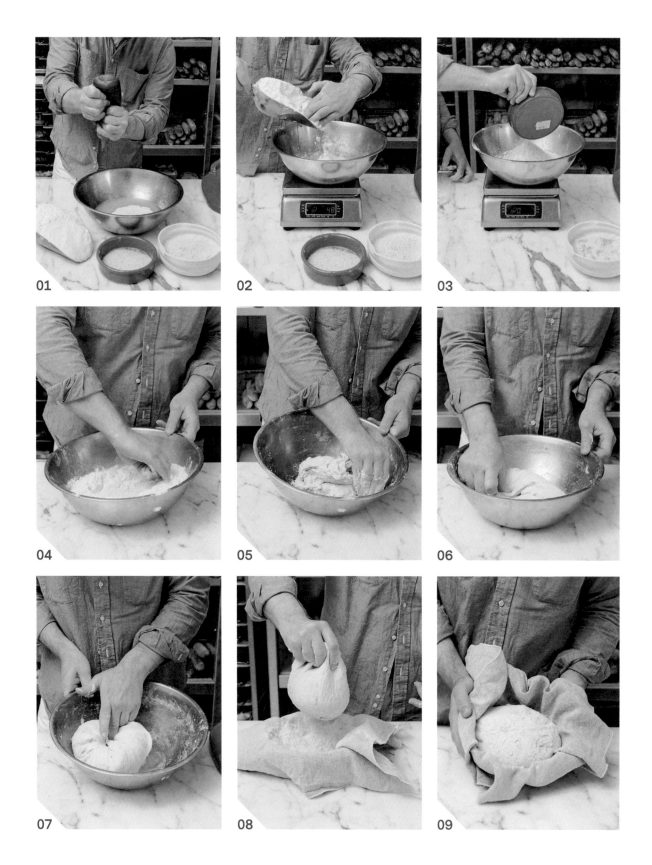

4. Hold onto the bowl with your clean hand and then, with the fingertips of your mixing hand, start making small circles in the centre of the bowl (image 04). (As a right-handed baker, I hold the mixing bowl with my left hand and use my right hand as the mixing tool, that way I always have one clean hand and one dirty hand; if you are left-handed, do the opposite.) After a couple of rotations, extend the circle to grab all the unincorporated dry bits on the sides of the bowl and bring them into the middle. Keep using your fingertips, not your palm.

5. When things are starting to come together, the dough will still look a bit scraggly, which is fine. We are not yet developing a dough, just forming the dough mix. Once the ingredients have come together, start using your hand to squeeze the scraggly dough ball, spinning the bowl around slowly with your free hand (image 05). Alternate between squeezing the dough and doing the revolutions with your hand. We are now starting to work the gluten. Continue this for 4–5 minutes until there are no more dry scraggly parts and you've formed a fairly uniform ball.

6. Now, start lifting the edges of the dough and folding them back over and into the centre (image 06). With each fold, continue to turn the bowl slowly. After one revolution, and about 8–10 folds, the dough will resemble the base of a round dumpling. With this dumpling method, you are speeding up the stretching and folding method; in fact, you are recreating your own version of a mechanical mixing bowl. Continue this lifting, stretching and rotating for 2–3 minutes. You should notice the elasticity of the dough change even in this short space of time.

7. Cover the bowl with a pizza tray and leave the dough to rest for 15 minutes. Repeat your homespun mechanical mixing bowl process. With your mixing hand, continue to lift and fold the dough into the centre while your clean hand rotates the bowl. Do this for another 5 minutes. When you're finished, scrape down your mixing hand and the side of the bowl with a dough scraper to get any stray bits. The dough should look slightly shiny, a bit loose and a little bit lumpy in texture.

BULK FERMENTATION

1. Cover the mixing bowl with the pizza tray and leave the dough somewhere relatively warm with a consistent temperature for 1.5 hours to rest and rise.

2. Remove the tray and give the dough another series of lift and folds, giving the bowl two full rotations. You should notice a big difference in the strength of the dough, and it should feel smoother and more elastic.

3. Scrape down the sides of the bowl again, then cover it with the pizza tray and leave the dough to rest, again in a warm place, for another 1.5–2 hours.

SHAPING

1. Shaping requires just as much attention and intuition as the other steps. You don't want to shape your loaf if the dough isn't ready for it; if you shape it too early, it can affect the final loaf composition and oven spring, that magnificent rise that comes with a well-proofed dough. If it's underproofed, it simply will not have developed enough strength to become a big, beautiful, aerated loaf.

    At the end of the bulk fermentation, the dough should have increased in volume by almost a third and look and feel elastic. It should seem full of life, with a gassy, billowy appearance, and be almost dome-like in shape. If it's dormant and unresponsive when you poke it, and it's not bouncing back, then it's underproofed and needs a bit longer. If you're still unsure, you can do a test similar to the starter-readiness test: tear off a tiny piece from the edge of the dough and place it in a small cup of water; if it floats, it's ready.

2. Start shaping by repeating the lift and fold technique in the bowl (image 07). Keep rotating the bowl and folding until you've stretched the dough into a ball that has enough tension that you can almost get your hand under it.

3. With the dough scraper, ease the dough out of the bowl, turning it out onto a bench dusted lightly with flour. You want the folds or seams of the loaf touching the floured bench and the smooth dome air-side up. Rest the loaf momentarily while you prepare your proofing basket.

4. Ricotta baskets are the ultimate proofing basket. Take a tea towel or cloth, place it in the basket and dust it with your dusting mix (see page 28).

5. Now come back to your loaf. Pick it up with both hands, then let the bulk of it drape down into the bowl, releasing it so it folds over onto itself. Now pick it back up, placing it on the bench with the seam down.

6. Pick the dough up again, place it in one hand, then use your other hand to rotate the dough 90 degrees, tucking the sides of the loaf underneath as you go. If you're right-handed, rotate with your right hand and gather with your left. Imagine the loaf as an upside-down dumpling, with the folded creases on the bottom and the smooth surface on top. As you pull the sides underneath, you'll create tension in the loaf, and it should end up creating a ball (or boule) shape. (If you've baked before you might have done this step by dragging the dough across the bench, but I prefer to use my hands because it's gentler on the dough.) You'll need to do about 6–10 rotations to get this shape.

7. Place the shaped loaf into your dusted cloth-lined basket with the creases facing up and the domed side on the bottom (image 08). Fold the edges of the cloth over the loaf to cover it.

8. Rest the loaf at room temperature for 1 hour, then transfer to the bottom of your fridge, where you'd normally keep your vegetables. This is the warmest part of your fridge, so clear a space here, even if it means pulling out your crisper drawer so the basket can sit there on an even surface. Now your final proofing process begins.

→

FINAL PROOFING

1. This is the make-or-bake phase for all the beautiful ingredients and focused energy you put into the mixing and shaping. A perfect proofing process doesn't always come off; this part is about instinct, which develops over time.

   For this final stage, the minimum time at the bottom of your fridge should be 12 hours, but I prefer 18 hours. Proofing the loaf in the fridge slows down the fermentation process – it's called 'retarding' in the baking world – increasing flavour and adding colour to the crust.

2. After it's spent the required time in the fridge, you'll need to create a window of time for your loaf to talk to you. This means taking it out of the fridge 4 hours before you bake, so that it has 3 hours to come to room temperature and show you its true colours before baking. Place the loaf in a mildly warm part of the house for 3 hours. It's during this next period that you need to be attuned to the calling cards of your dough telling you that it's ready.

Look for:

- **The Proofing:** The dome-like shape, the billowiness of the loaf. The loaf should be perky in appearance, but not too perky.

- **The Tension:** Is the loaf holding its shape, or is it kind of collapsing and oozing all over? You want shape.

- **The Feel:** It should be gassy and aerated, but spring back at a light touch.

When a loaf is overproofed, the dough will look gassy and bulging, almost on the verge of collapse. If you bake it like this, it can result in a deflated pancake instead of a nice loaf. If you don't, however, it's not a complete failure, since you can make focaccia with it instead (see page 61).

At the other end of the spectrum, if it's underproofed the resulting loaf will be like a tight balloon and be too tight and tough in texture. In this case, give it a bit longer at room temperature.

BAKING

1. Once you've had the loaf out of the fridge for 2 hours, start heating the oven and Dutch oven. This is the most crucial step. When I say heat, I mean grab the temperature dial and turn it all the way up to 250°C (480°F), or as high as your oven goes, even if that's higher. Don't turn on the fan.

2. Place your Dutch oven in the oven with the lid on and set a timer. It should take 40 minutes for everything to get roaring hot.

3. By now, the dough should be at hour 3 of proofing at room temperature. Still, that doesn't mean you just throw the loaf in the oven; look for all the signs mentioned opposite to see if the loaf is ready and, if needed, wait a bit longer, checking it at 15-minute intervals.

4. Once it's ready (image 09), you'll need to move quickly, so preparation is key: have a sheet of baking paper as wide as your Dutch oven (or even 2.5 cm/an inch wider) ready. This will be your landing pad after you take your loaf out of its basket. Have your chosen scoring tool within easy reach.

5. When the oven is roaring hot and the loaf looks ready to go, gently tip the loaf out from the basket onto the baking paper, so that the seam of the loaf is lying flat on the baking paper and the dome-shaped side is facing up.

6. Score the loaf using your blade. Less is more with scoring, and the loaf will again dictate to you what happens. (If the loaf is sitting up and not so relaxed, you may even want to think about resting it up to another hour longer.) If you feel confident in the loaf's condition, then go ahead and score. If the loaf is well-and-truly ripe and is feeling like a jellyfish, take it easy on the scoring – perhaps give it only a single delicate score down the middle or a light cross in the centre of the loaf. If it's less relaxed and still looks quite tight even after you've rested it for longer, then score it a little more deeply to give it room to expand during baking.

7. Once the loaf is scored, place a wooden board or heatproof trivet on the bench, slip on your oven mitts, and pull the Dutch oven out, being sure to close the oven door quickly. Place the pot on the board, then remove the lid. Gripping the edges of the baking paper, pick up the loaf and lower it gently yet quickly into the Dutch oven. Replace the lid and place the pot into your hot oven once more.

8. Bake for 30–40 minutes with the lid on, then remove the Dutch oven from the oven (again using mitts) and remove the lid. Place the pot, uncovered, back into the oven for a minimum of 30 minutes. This will give the loaf colour and flavour.

    Here is where you call the shots on what you desire in terms of crust and colour. I prefer a dark crust, so I bake it for 40 minutes with the lid on, then 40 minutes with the lid off. When you achieve the colour you desire, remove the pot from the oven, lift the loaf out and pick it up with oven mitts. To check it's done, tap the base with your knuckle. It should sound like a door being knocked.

9. Place your baked loaf on a wire cooling rack. Resist as long as possible before slicing it (at least 30 minutes): slicing into a hot loaf will reduce the shelf life of the bread and contribute to it becoming dry.

Olive and walnut loaf

MAKES A 1.2 KG (2 LB 12 OZ) LOAF

This loaf takes the basic country loaf recipe (page 46) and adds a delicious mix of black and green olives and the crunch of walnuts. The hydration and salt has also been adjusted to counter the brininess of the olives.

In fact, this is one of our all-time favourite loaves. Unfortunately, we had to take it off the shelves at Baker Bleu, since it wasn't affordable for us to make at the standard we wanted. Thankfully, we can share it here.

We like to eat this bread both fresh or a few days old and toasted with a cheese board. We hope it finds a place in your bread basket.

BAKING INGREDIENTS AND PERCENTAGES		
Ripe starter (page 36)	130 g (4½ oz)	30%
Strong (baker's) flour	300 g (10½ oz)	70%
Wholemeal stoneground emmer flour	130 g (4½ oz)	30%
Filtered water, at 28°C (82°F)	310 g (11 oz)	72%
Barley (or rice) malt syrup	5 g (⅛ oz)	1%
Pitted olives (mix of Kalamata and Manzanilla), well drained	195 g (6¾ oz)	45%
Activated walnuts (organic, or best available), coarsely chopped	150 g (5½ oz)	35%
Torn rosemary leaves	9 g (¼ oz)	2%
Fine pink salt	9.5 g (¼ oz)	2.2%

1. Follow the directions to prep your starter given in the country loaf recipe (page 46), then follow the method for the country loaf up to step 3 of mixing, but using the ingredients listed above and holding back a tablespoon or so of water. Once you've added the flour, follow it with the olives, walnuts and rosemary. If the dough looks a little dry at this point, add the remaining water. Continue mixing as per the country loaf recipe.

2. Proceed as you would for the standard country loaf until you're ready to bake, keeping in mind that when it comes to stretching and folding, you may need to use smaller movements than you would with the country loaf due to the olives and walnuts, which make the dough a little more dense.

3. Following that same country loaf method, bake the loaf for 30 minutes with the lid on and 30 minutes with the lid off, then leave to cool on a wire rack as per the same recipe.

NOTE

Adding the olives and walnuts when we do gives their full impact to the bread, both flavour-wise and colour-wise, where they'll give the dough a beautiful purple hue.

Growing Pains

Every job has its unglamorous side. Running a bakery, though, can be particularly rough. It's essentially manual labour. Your body is on the line.

At our first bakery, I would spend so long in front of our tiny oven that my eyes would become bloodshot and the hair on my arms and legs was scorched by the heat radiating off that thing. I even developed something called burning mouth syndrome. On Fridays, when we baked challah, there were only four hours out of 24 that I wouldn't be at the bakery.

At the end of a long day of baking, sometimes I would head down to Elwood Beach and throw myself into the water. It didn't matter if it was winter and it was only me and the labradors that were crazy enough to swim. The freezing water felt amazing after 12 hours beside an oven.

Around this time, Mia frequently felt dizzy because she was always on the move, trying to do the jobs of four people.

There were some days in our first year of business when it was truly miserable. There was no separation between back of house and front of house. People could see everything we were doing, and we could hear everything they were saying.

Customers weren't afraid to share their opinions, and they had plenty of suggestions for us.

'Why don't you do gluten-free bread?'

'You should do sandwiches!'

'Can't you bake more, if you sell out each day?'

'Why don't you make coffee?'

A gentleman came in one day for some bagels, took one look around and said, in a prophetic kind of tone as he doffed his hat, 'This site is cursed. You will not survive here, but your business will thrive.'

We were both so tired and everything felt really raw.

But then we'd get the kids of customers bringing in drawings they'd done of the bakery because they loved visiting every day. Or they'd make up songs about the bakery and sing them to you.

Opening our second bakery was literally DIY, because we had no money for builders. We had to spend it all on baking equipment.

Getting bigger didn't necessarily take away any pressure. Opening our second bakery was literally DIY, because we had no money for builders. We had to spend it all on baking equipment.

I would bake at our original shop from 2am or 3am, then head over to the second bakery we were building at 7am and work on the tools with Mia's dad all day. At 5pm, we'd head home. I'd shower immediately (if I sat down, I'd fall asleep), mix a Negroni, eat whatever Mia's mum had cooked for dinner and usually find myself with my eyes closed a few minutes later with my phone still lit up in my hand.

At one point, Mia was on crutches and I had my arm in a sling because we'd injured ourselves working on the build for the new bakery.

These are the things no one tells you in their story about chasing their dreams.

Rye-caraway loaf

MAKES A 1.2 KG (2 LB 12 OZ) LOAF

This dough is a light rye, so it has a mild flavour but still boasts a beautiful scent, matched perfectly with the caraway seeds we add. It's a good one for sandwiches, such as the curried egg on page 204, or small bites with oily or salty things on top. The beef tartare tapa on page 189 is a great example of those flavours working together.

Rye doughs can be sticky to handle and require more gentle mixing. Doing a few extra folds on your dough will alleviate this. We also use cold water, rather than room temperature. Rye grain is quite high in nutrients and fermentable sugars, so it's naturally more active; cold water gives you more control over the dough's activity.

BAKING INGREDIENTS AND PERCENTAGES		
Ripe starter (page 36)	175 g (6 oz)	30%
Strong (baker's) flour	410 g (14½)	70%
Whole rye stoneground flour	175 g	30%
Filtered water, at 15°C (60°F)	420 g	72%
Barley (or rice) malt syrup	6 g	1%
Caraway seeds	15 g	2.6%
Fine pink salt	16 g	2.7%

1. Follow the directions to prep your starter and mix your dough given in the country loaf recipe (page 46), but using the ingredients listed above and adding the caraway seeds after the flour.

2. Continue as you would for the standard country loaf but, at step 6 of the mixing, add another full revolution of 8–10 folds.

3. Proceed as you would normally for the country loaf, baking the loaf for 30 minutes with the lid on and 30 minutes with the lid off, then leave to cool on a wire rack as per the same recipe.

Seeded spelt loaf

MAKES A 1.2 KG (2 LB 12 OZ) LOAF

Packed with tasty seeds and grains, this is one of our best-selling loaves. It's amazing when it's used for a salad sandwich, it makes a mean egg sandwich and I love it for chicken and mayo sandwiches. But it's amazing simply toasted and spread with peanut butter, too.

In total this recipe uses a full batch of seeded spelt mix, which is detailed in the pantry recipes section on page 222. Hold back the salt, split the mix in two, then add half the mix to the loaf, reserving the rest (which is then salted) for coating.

BAKING INGREDIENTS AND PERCENTAGES		
Ripe starter (page 36)	140 g (5 oz)	30%
Strong (baker's) flour	230 g (8 oz)	50%
Spelt or stoneground emmer flour	230 g (8 oz)	50%
Filtered water, at 28°C (82°F)	345 g (12 oz)	75%
Honey	45 g (1¾ oz)	10%
Barley (or rice) malt syrup	5 g (⅛ oz)	1%
Seeded spelt mix (page 222), salt omitted	200 g (7 oz)	43%
Fine pink salt	12 g (¼ oz)	2.6%

EXTRA INGREDIENTS

200 g (7 oz) seeded spelt mix (page 222)

1. Follow the directions to prep your starter, mix your dough and bulk ferment your loaf given in the country loaf recipe (page 46), but using the ingredients above, adding the honey with the malt syrup and the seeded spelt mix after the flour.

2. Follow the shaping steps, stopping before you put your shaped loaf into its proofing basket.

3. Let your shaped loaf sit on your bench while you prepare a small plate or tray with a wet (saturated) tea towel on it. Place a low-sided tray big enough to hold your loaf next to it, and fill it with the salted seed mix.

4. Roll your loaf in its entirety (even the bottom) over the wet kitchen cloth, then roll it through the seed mix. Make sure you coat the whole loaf.

5. Follow the final two steps of the shaping process, followed by the final proofing process in the country loaf recipe.

6. After the overnight rest, heat the oven to 250°C (480°F), or as high as it goes, and follow the same baking process. Note that you will need to reduce the bake time, due to the honey and natural sugars of this loaf. Reduce the bake time to 20 minutes with the lid on followed by 20 minutes with it off.

7. Remove the loaf from the oven and transfer it to a wire cooling rack. Resist as long as possible before slicing it (at least 30 minutes).

NOTE

Any excess seeds can go into your health cracker recipe (page 216).

Deep-dish focaccia

MAKES A 1.2 KG (2 LB 12 OZ) FOCACCIA OR 2 x 600 G (1 LB 5 OZ) FOCACCIAS,
SERVING 4–6 PEOPLE (A PORTION EACH)

EXTRA EQUIPMENT

For 1 large focaccia:
Gastronorm pan,
325 x 265 mm
(13 x 10½ inches)
with a depth of 65 mm
(2½ inches)

For 2 focaccias:
Gastronorm pans x 2,
265 x 162 mm
(10½ x 6¼ inches)
with a depth of 65 mm
(2½ inches)

There's nothing more rewarding than a bang-for-buck recipe, and this focaccia – made with the exact same dough as you prepare for your country loaf – is one of them.

Essentially, it's a super-hydrated levain dough, which means when you put it into a deep-dish pan with loads of olive oil, you're going to get fluffy, moreish focaccia – nothing like the sad, dry versions you might remember from the 1990s.

I learned that you could take country loaf dough and produce focaccia from it while I was working at Iggy's in Sydney. I instantly thought it was amazing. You proof it for the same length of time as a loaf, so you get that super-developed flavour, and you're just sitting a slab of dough in a tray, so there's no shaping needed.

In the early days of Baker Bleu, we couldn't bake enough loaves of bread for all our customers, so we filled the gap by doing focaccia. We could just pop the dough in a huge container to proof in the coolroom and didn't have to take up space with more loaves in the proofing rack.

That sort of ease is also perfect for home bakers; if you're having friends over and you wanted to make some bread, this is it. And it's the perfect dinner accompaniment, perfect for schmearing through all the leftovers on the plate.

Italians are so traditional: focaccia must be a certain size, especially if you're from Liguria. This is more freestyle, more Anglo-American.

It definitely won't be dry because it's deep-dish. And because there's so much dough content, there's opportunity to add ingredients. Some favourites of mine are rosemary and sea salt, olives, or roasted or raw onion, which I find really elevate the whole thing, especially with the crisp crusts you get.

A rosemary and sea salt version, which is detailed on page 62, is exceptional with mortadella and stracciatella sandwiches, served alongside roasted capsicums (peppers) or soft cheese, or paired with any type of cured meat.

One final note: the quality of your olive oil really matters here, since it's one of only three ingredients giving the bread its flavour. Buy the best you can afford and use it for dishes like this where it will steal the show.

NOTE

The key to great focaccia is depth. Don't bake it in too large a pan or the bread will end up too shallow. A Dutch oven is too deep.

→

INGREDIENTS

1 quantity of country loaf ingredients (page 46)

¼ cup (60 ml) good-quality extra-virgin olive oil

2 rosemary sprigs, picked and very finely chopped

Large pinch of sea salt flakes

1. Follow the recipe to prepare your country loaf dough (page 46) up until the end of the bulk fermentation. Now, instead of shaping the loaf into a ball, we're going to let the dough naturally expand into the shape of our baking pan or tray.

2. Take the gastronorm pan (or pans) and smear a third of the oil on the inside, getting into every nook and cranny and making sure you do the sides and edges, too. If you're using two pans, split the oil evenly between each.

3. Lay your proofed dough into the pan, then stretch it gently into each corner. Don't force it. Use your fingertips to caress it from the middle to the edges, then lift and ease the underside of the dough so it drapes over the sides of the pan. Let the dough rest for 5–10 minutes (it'll shrink back), then repeat the stretching. In total, you want to stretch the dough to fit the pan four times, remembering to let it rest in between.

4. Once you're happy that the dough has been stretched to fill all areas of the pan, allow it to rest for 3–4 hours at room temperature. Alternatively, you can rest it overnight (12 hours) in the lowest part of the fridge, then for 6 hours at room temperature. In both circumstances, cover the pan with a tea towel.

5. In the final hour of proofing, heat the oven to 240°C (475°F). Once the oven is at temperature, it's time to dress your focaccia. Drizzle most of the remaining oil over the dough as evenly as possible. With the flat of your hand, massage the oil over the top, then ease the sides of the dough away from the edges of the baking pan and drizzle a little more oil on the dough. This step helps ensure the focaccia comes out of the pan easily after baking.

6. Garnish the dough with the rosemary, covering the entire surface evenly. Do the same with the sea salt flakes. Be generous – the toppings are everything!

7. Now comes the fun part. With the tips of your fingers, make dimples in the dough across the whole surface. This gives focaccia its trademark appearance.

8. Bake the focaccia for 35–40 minutes until blistered, golden and a burnished dark brown in places. Remove from the oven and let cool in the pan for 10 minutes, then ease out with a spatula onto a wire cooling rack.

VARIATIONS

At step 6, instead of garnishing with rosemary and sea salt, you can try one of these variations:

OLIVE AND ROSEMARY FOCACCIA

Drizzle the focaccia with 2 tablespoons extra-virgin olive oil (use 1 tablespoon for each focaccia if you're baking two small focaccias) and use the back of your hand to massage it over the surface. Measure out 1 cup (160 g) of pitted Manzanilla olives and 1 cup (150 g) pitted Kalamata olives, and depress the whole olives into the dough. Use your fingers to dimple any unfilled parts of the dough, then finish by scattering it with two very finely chopped rosemary sprigs and plenty of sea salt flakes. Bake as per the core recipe.

ROASTED ONION FOCACCIA

At least 3 hours before baking, heat the oven to 110°C (225°F). Place two whole brown onions – skins and all – on a baking tray and roast them for an hour; do not use any oil. Remove, then allow them to cool completely (about an hour; or leave them overnight in the fridge).

When you're ready to dress the focaccia, measure out 2 tablespoons extra-virgin olive oil and finely chop two rosemary sprigs.

Drizzle half the oil over the dough, and massage it over the surface of the focaccia. Peel the onion skins and remove any elements of the root. Begin to peel the onion's layers away. As you go, use each layer to make a depression in the surface of the dough, pressing it into the body of the dough. Continue this process across the focaccia until it's fairly well covered; feel free to add more onion if you want more flavour. Drizzle the remaining olive oil evenly across the dough, then sprinkle with rosemary and a generous amount of sea salt flakes. Bake as per the core recipe.

Olive fougasse

MAKES 2 x 600 G (1 LB 5 OZ) FOUGASSES

Fougasse is underrated. At home, with drinks before dinner we always have dips and antipasti boards. This is where fougasse shines. It's a great centrepiece with an interesting shape that people aren't afraid to rip up.

Tear off a length of the bread, dip one side in hummus, the other in some baba ghanoush – you'll be thinking to yourself, 'Life is good.' Of course, you can also eat fougasse on its own, especially when you flavour it like we have here.

We love to use two varieties of olives. Most frequently we use Kalamata and Gordal olives.

I hadn't eaten much fougasse before we started selling it, which happened one day because of a baking mishap when one of our mixers made up three country loaf dough recipes with only 10 per cent starter. The dough was totally lifeless, so we rested it overnight in bulk, stretched it out the next day and baked it, and were surprised at how well the bread came up with such little effort. Since then, we've honed it, and it's now a fixture at Baker Bleu.

BAKING INGREDIENTS AND PERCENTAGES		
Ripe starter (page 36)	155 g (5½ oz)	30%
Strong (baker's) flour	470 g (1 lb 1 oz)	90%
Spelt flour	50 g (1¾ oz)	10%
Filtered water, at 28°C (82°F)	340 g (12 oz)	65%
Barley (or rice) malt syrup	5 g (⅛ oz)	1%
Chopped fresh rosemary	2 g (¹⁄₁₆ oz)	0.5%
Fine pink salt	11 g (¼ oz)	2.2%
Whole pitted olives (see note)	180 g (6½ oz)	35%

EXTRA INGREDIENTS

Sunflower oil, for greasing
Extra-virgin olive oil, for brushing

1. Follow the directions to prep your starter given in the country loaf recipe (page 46), then add the water, starter and malt syrup to your mixing bowl, followed by the flours, rosemary, salt and two-thirds of the olives, being sure to keep the salt away from the starter.

2. Begin mixing with your hand from the centre, slowly bringing the outside ingredients in towards the middle of the bowl. Work the mixture, keeping one hand rotating the bowl and the other one mixing the dough, until you have a dough that is beginning to feel elastic (approximately 3 minutes).

→

3. Incorporate the remaining olives, and begin shaping the dough using the dumpling folding technique specified in the country loaf recipe (see step 6 on page 48). Continue this for 2–3 minutes.

4. Rest the fougasse dough at room temperature, covered with a pizza tray, for 30 minutes, then do another 2 minutes of stretches and folds.

5. Lightly oil the sides of your bowl with sunflower oil to help the dough come away more easily, then cover the dough again and leave at room temperature for 1.5 hours to rest.

6. Repeat another round of stretches and folds.

7. Rest the dough, covered, for another 1.5 hours. At the end of this, you can either refrigerate the dough overnight at the bottom of your fridge (where the crisper lives), or you can proof it in a warm spot for 3 hours.

8. If you have refrigerated overnight, remove your dough and let it come to room temperature over the course of 3 hours. An hour before you want to bake, heat the oven to 250°C (480°F), or its maximum temperature. Line a large rectangular baking tray (the largest you have) with baking paper.

9. Without putting any tension into the dough, transfer it to a heavily floured chopping board. Don't scoop the dough out of the bowl; tip the bowl and let it drape onto the board. Divide your dough into two equal pieces of approximately 600 g (1 lb 5 oz). Cover these with a tea towel and leave to rest for 15–20 minutes.

10. Transfer one piece of dough to the baking tray, where you'll stretch it out. To do so, put your hands on the underside of the dough and gently stretch it outwards. You want to elongate the dough, stretching it to about double its length, but being careful not to overstretch it or make it super thin.

11. Take your dough scraper and make 3–4 punctures in the dough, going all the way in with the edge and jiggling the scraper to cut through. Now use your fingers to gently fan out the holes so they have small strips of dough between them. Do this quickly.

12. Immediately place the tray in the oven and bake for 25–30 minutes. (Leave the other fougasse resting under a tea towel until it's ready to bake.) Remove the first fougasse from the oven and brush it with extra-virgin olive oil, then transfer to a wire cooling rack to cool briefly; this is best served warm. As it cools, repeat the stretching and cutting of the dough for the second fougasse and put it in to bake, ready for when you finish polishing off the first.

NOTE

We like to use first-batch, pitted olives from Mount Zero in Victoria. We add them whole because they get squelched together and torn up in the mixing, adding much stronger flavour and colour to the dough. The second quantity of olives, which don't get so broken down, are added for aesthetics.

VARIATIONS

To make a simple **sea salt-rosemary fougasse**, follow the recipe above but add another 2 g (1/16 oz) of chopped rosemary when you'd otherwise add the second batch of olives. Finish with another sprinkle of sea salt after brushing the hot fougasse with olive oil.

For **roasted onion fougasse**, roast 1–2 whole brown onions (depending on how much you like onion) in their skins in a low oven (150°C/300°F) for an hour, without any oil. Let them cool, roughly chop them (skin and all), then add them to the dough in place of the olives.

Cherry-chocolate bread

MAKES 10 BUNS OR 2 x 600 G (1 LB 5 OZ) LOAVES

The first Easter that Baker Bleu was open we thought about how we would attempt to do a hot-cross bun that was distinctly our own, with dried cherries for that dried-fruit Easter feeling, and good dark chocolate because, well, chocolate. Some say chocolate is a crime against hot cross buns, but we think it's delicious in this guise, especially when you slather the bread with plenty of butter.

Mixing in whole ingredients from the very start gives you hunks of chocolate and cherry of all different sizes throughout the bread.

BAKING INGREDIENTS AND PERCENTAGES		
Filtered water, at 28°C (82°F)	285 g (10 oz)	71%
Ripe starter (page 36)	100 g (3½ oz)	25%
Dried yeast	1 g (¹⁄₁₆ oz)	0.25%
Barley (or rice) malt syrup	4 g (⅛ oz)	1%
Strong (baker's) flour	400 g (14 oz)	100%
Caster (superfine) sugar	12 g (¼ oz)	3%
Fine pink salt	10 g (¼ oz)	2.5%
Ground cinnamon	4 g (⅛ oz)	1%
Good-quality dark (70%) chocolate	140 g (5 oz)	35%
Dried cherries, soaked in apple juice (see note)	180 g (6½ oz)	45%

1. Add the water, starter (feed it and check it as per the preparing your starter section in the country loaf recipe on page 46), yeast and malt syrup to your large mixing bowl, then add the flour, sugar, salt (keep it away from the starter and yeast) and cinnamon. Roughly break up the chocolate with your hands and add it to the bowl, along with the cherries.

2. This dough requires a little more effort to mix as you will be crushing the ingredients together by hand. With one hand securing the bowl, start mixing from the centre of the bowl, gradually bringing the outer ingredients into the middle, then incorporating everything until it starts to resemble a shaggy mix.

3. Continue mixing, a little more vigorously to develop the dough, crushing the large pieces of chocolate and cherries in your hand as you work the dough. Continue for 10 minutes.

NOTE

Dried cherries that haven't been soaked in apple juice will be too dry for this recipe. Try and seek out the apple-soaked (or 'apple juice sweetened') variety from health-food shops or grocers. If you can't find them, soak the cherries yourself in apple juice for 1 hour, then drain and use.

➜

4. Lift and fold the dough in the same dumpling style as for the country loaf recipe (see step 6 on page 48). Cover the dough with a pizza tray, leave it at room temperature for 30 minutes to rest, then repeat the lifting and folding two more times, with 30 minutes rest in between.

5. After the third series of lifts and folds, bulk ferment the dough (see page 48), covered, for 1.5 hours in an ambient place.

6. Repeat two full rotations of lifting and folding, then rest for a further 1.5 hours. The total bulk fermentation time is 3 hours.

7. Now, it's time to choose whether you want to make two trays of cherry chocolate buns or two loaves. Coax the dough out of the bowl onto a lightly floured bench. Gently form the dough into a rectangle with your hands, then, depending on whether you want to make buns or loaves, divide the dough with your pastry card. For buns, you want to divide the rectangle into 10 equal pieces of dough weighing approximately 100 g (3½ oz). For loaves, simply halve the rectangle.

8. Prepare two baking trays (for the buns) by lining each with paper, or prepare two ricotta baskets (for the loaves) by lining each with a floured tea towel.

9. For both the loaves and the buns, the shape to aim for is round. To shape the buns, roll each piece of dough into a ball and place on the baking tray, a few centimetres apart. For the boule-shaped loaves, use the shaping method described from step 5 of the shaping section on page 49 of the country loaf recipe. Once shaped, place each loaf seam-side up in the basket.

10. You can either bake on the same day or rest the dough overnight for even more flavour. For the same-day method, rest the dough for 3 hours, covered, in an ambient place. For the overnight method, place the ricotta baskets or trays in the bottom part of your fridge (where the crisper lives) for 12 hours, ensuring the dough is covered with the tea towel. The next day, remove the dough from the fridge 3 hours before you want to bake.

11. One hour before you want to bake, heat the oven to 250°C (480°F).

12. If baking buns, brush them with water and bake them on the baking tray for 20 minutes. If baking loaves, preheat your Dutch oven, as per the country loaf recipe (see page 51). After an hour, remove the Dutch oven carefully. Gently tip out your boule from your ricotta basket onto baking paper, so the seam is on the bottom. Score the loaf with a square or cross and lower it into the Dutch oven using the baking paper to help you. Replace the lid and return to the oven. Bake for 20 minutes with the lid on, followed by 20 minutes with the lid off. Repeat for the second loaf.

13. Once the buns or loaves are ready, remove from the oven and cool on a wire rack.

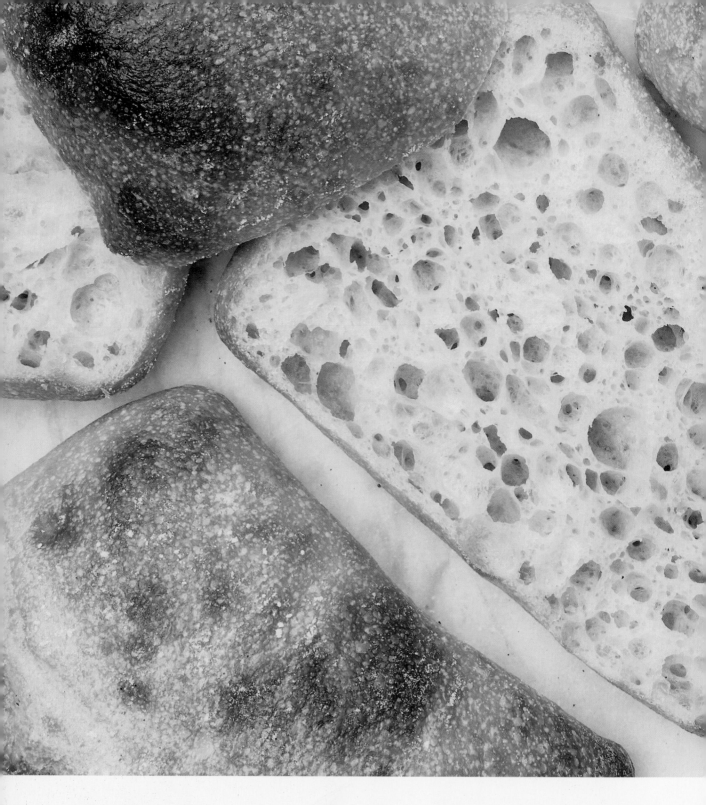

Ciabatta & Panini

Ciabatta and Panini

MAKES 2 x 600 G (1 LB 5 OZ) LOAVES, OR ABOUT 6 PANINI

Ciabatta's literal translation is 'slipper'. It's a crisp bread with a soft, aerated interior, but it has a much harder exterior than many of the other breads in this book.

We started baking ciabatta at our first shop because, again, we needed to offer more bread to our growing number of customers and we didn't have any space to proof more of our standard loaves. Ciabatta is a fantastic recipe because you can bulk ferment it in big tubs overnight, which is partly what makes it the style of bread it is. If you choose to also then rest it overnight, you'll be rewarded with more flavour.

I think this is the perfect sandwich bread: it holds things well but isn't too hard to chew. With this core recipe, you can choose to make ciabatta loaves or panini, or you can take things up a notch with my take on stirato, inspired by baker Jim Lahey's recipe, in which the long, baguette-shaped loaves are studded with tasty things. As you'll see in the following pages, it's a dough that lends itself well to pizza, too.

I'll warn you, though: ciabatta and panini have a same-day shelf life. Bake the day you want to eat.

BAKING INGREDIENTS AND PERCENTAGES		
Ripe starter (page 36)	165 g (5¾ oz)	30%
Strong (baker's) flour	545 g (1 lb 3 oz)	100%
Filtered water, at 28°C (82°F)	410 g (14½ oz)	75%
Extra-virgin olive oil	50 g (1¾ oz)	9%
Barley (or rice) malt syrup	6 g (⅛ oz)	1%
Fine pink salt	14 g (½ oz)	2.6%

1. Follow the directions to prep your starter and mix your dough given in the country loaf recipe (page 46), but using the ingredients above, adding the oil with the malt syrup. Stop at the bulk fermentation stage – this part is a little more laborious for ciabatta since the ciabatta dough is very wet – and follow one of the methods over the page, depending on whether you want to make same-day or let it go overnight, which will give a more complex result.

→

SAME-DAY CIABATTA

1. To fold the dough, imagine it's a handkerchief and fold all the edges (still in the bowl) into the centre. Do this every 30 minutes for the next 3 hours, covering it with a pizza tray and leaving it at room temperature between foldings. It will resemble the base of a dumpling once complete.

2. After you've done six rounds of folding and resting, let the dough rest in the bowl, covered, for a final 3 hours. You'll then be ready to portion the dough.

OVERNIGHT CIABATTA

1. To fold the dough, imagine it's a handkerchief and fold all the edges (still in the bowl) into the centre. Do this every 30 minutes for the next 3 hours, covering it with a pizza tray and leaving it at room temperature between foldings. It will resemble the base of a dumpling once complete.

2. After you've done six rounds of folding and resting, transfer the dough from the bowl to a 2-litre (8 cup) plastic container and place it immediately in the bottom part of the fridge (where the crisper lives) for 24 hours to rest. Allow 3 hours for the dough to come up to room temperature before you move to the next step.

SHAPING AND BAKING

1. After the dough has rested, either at room temperature or in the fridge, then come to room temperature, prepare a bench for shaping and dividing the dough: dust it lightly with flour and get your pastry card ready.

2. Scrape out the dough onto the bench and stretch it gently from each corner to create a rectangle. With your ricotta basket or sifter, sift flour over the surface of the dough, then use your hands to gently stretch and depress the dough to create an even surface. The final rectangle should be about 3–4 cm (1¼–1½ inches) thick and roughly 29 x 22 cm (11½ x 8 ½ inches).

3. To make ciabatta loaves, simply halve the rectangle with your pastry card and transfer each strip or log to a baking tray lined with baking paper. Cover the loaves with a tea towel.

    To make panini, you are going to cut smaller pieces of dough off the rectangular strips. Aim for 180 g (6½ oz) per piece of dough (you can use a scale to guide you). Don't be limited by what shape you cut off: you can do smaller squares, rectangles, circles or triangles, but do try to keep a uniform shape and weight so they bake evenly. Place each piece of dough onto a lined baking tray and cover with a tea towel.

4. Heat the oven to 250°C (480°F), or as high as it will go. The time it takes for the oven to heat will be the perfect intermediate proofing time for your ciabatta or panini, which is roughly 45–60 minutes.

5. Once the dough has rested and the oven is preheated, bake for 30 minutes (regardless of whether you're making loaves or panini), rotating the trays halfway through to ensure even colour. Cool briefly on a wire rack and eat the same day.

Stirato

MAKES 6

Stirato is almost like a focaccia, but instead of it baking in a deep tray, you're cutting your ciabatta dough into rectangular pieces and studding it with ingredients, such as green olives, small pieces of onion, crumbled chorizo, confit garlic, the list goes on. Just don't chop anything too small, otherwise it will get burnt.

I like to bake strips of these together on a tray, sometimes with different toppings, ready to pull apart when they come out of the oven. These are perfect as lunch on the run or a snack to serve with drinks.

INGREDIENTS

1 x quantity of ciabatta
    dough (page 74)
Olive oil, for greasing
Toppings of your choice,
    such as green olives,
    onion, chorizo or
    confit garlic

1. Follow the process for making the ciabatta dough (page 74) up to the end of step 2 of the shaping and baking section (like with the ciabatta, you can choose whether to follow the same-day or overnight method).

2. Use a pastry card or pizza cutter to cut strips off the rectangle of dough. Aim for six strips the length of the shorter side of your baking tray.

3. Grease the baking tray well with olive oil, then lay the ribbons of dough onto the tray and press the toppings into the dough so they stud the surface. My only advice here is to chop things evenly and distribute them evenly over the top of the dough; I like to stud them about 1 cm (½ inch) apart.

4. Heat the oven to 240°C (475°F), allowing the dough to rest for between 45 and 60 minutes as it heats up.

5. Once the dough has rested and the oven is hot, bake for 25 minutes, rotating the tray halfway through. Cool the stirato on a wire rack briefly before serving. Like the ciabatta itself, these are best eaten on the day of baking.

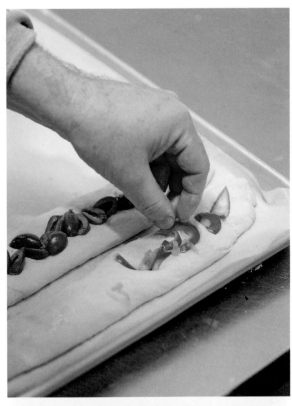

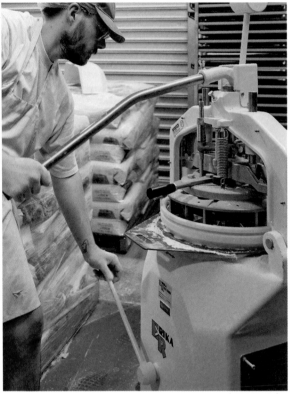

Pizza

MAKES 5 x 30 CM (12 INCH) ROUND PIZZAS

We love pizza at our bakeries. If a bakery produces naturally leavened dough and bakes on a stone hearth deck, in my opinion pizza is a non-negotiable. It's the world's best food. I don't even think it needs to be categorised into street food. It's simply food.

I love that can vary so much in style, depending on where you are: Neapolitan, Roman, deep dish, grandma… But the one constant I've found is that you must respect the dough formation and the resting process, and you must use killer ingredients.

Still, our dough is one of convenience. We bake ciabatta daily and this dough provides us with the perfect pizza base. It also keeps very well in the fridge, so you can make a batch on Sunday, and eat pizza again on Thursday or Friday. Similar to a Roman-style pizza, ours is crisp without being dry, has the goodness and complexity of a naturally leavened dough, and it's enriched with olive oil for a fuller flavour.

If you're lucky enough to have a compact pizza oven, such as a Gozney or Breville, you will get even better results.

INITIAL DOUGH

INGREDIENTS

1 x quantity of ciabatta dough (page 74)
Semolina flour, for dusting
Toppings (see page 85)

1. Follow the process for making the ciabatta dough (page 74) up to the start of the shaping and baking section (like with the ciabatta, you can choose whether to follow the same-day or overnight method).

2. Divide the dough into 5 x 240 g (8½ oz) pieces.

3. Now, you are going to shape each piece into a firm dough ball. To do this, use very lightly floured hands to form a dough ball in your hands (see step 6 of the shaping section in the country loaf recipe on page 46) so it becomes a tight ball, smooth on top and sealed on the bottom. You will probably need fewer rotations than with the country loaf since these pieces of dough are smaller.

4. Dust a proofing tray well with semolina, place each ball on the tray, then dust the tops and cover with a lid. Now you can go one of two ways.

SAME-DAY PIZZA:

Rest the dough balls for 12 hours at room temperature, ideally 24°C (75°F), until they have doubled in size. This dough gets better the more you rest it, so you can even rest it for up to 24 hours at room temperature and get great results.

→

PREPARE-AHEAD PIZZA:

Place the tray of dough balls in the fridge for at least 12 hours or up to 5 days, if you like the idea of having pizza at home on demand. A long, cold ferment will give you a super-bubbly, blistered crust. If you go with this approach, allow at least an hour for the dough to come to room temperature before baking.

BAKING

1. When you're ready to bake, remove all trays and shelves in your oven except for the bottom level. Place a pizza stone on the bottom shelf and heat the oven to 250°C (480°F), or its maximum temperature. Great pizza comes from super-hot ovens, so don't be afraid to crank it up.

2. While the oven is heating, get your pizza-topping station ready, with toppings prepped, sauces made and so on. You want this ready to go by the time you're stretching your dough because once you start this process, you don't want any delays or the pizza will stick and get dry.

3. In preparation for stretching, if your dough's been in the fridge, pull it out and bring it to room temperature for at least an hour or up to 8 hours. If the dough looks underproofed (use the poke test; it should bounce back if it's ready), keep resting it, covered, and check on it every 30 minutes.

4. To stretch pizza, I use three techniques, always focusing on maintaining a circle and never piercing the dough. The other thing is to make sure the smooth side of your dough ball faces upwards and the seam is underneath. You will get a better rise this way. First, flour the bench liberally and dust some flour on the top of your dough. Dock the dough (press it) with your fingertips, working from the centre outwards, avoiding piercing the dough. This should increase the size by two or three times.

5. Next, drape the dough by sliding your joined hands, palms facing down, underneath the dough and then pointing your fingertips downwards in an inverted prayer shape to lift the dough off the surface with the backs of your hands. You don't want your fingers anywhere near the dough or piercing it. Gently move your hands in opposite directions away from each other and carefully rotate the dough to stretch it evenly. At this point you can drop the dough and reapply some more flour, and make sure things are being stretched correctly and there are no thick clumpy areas of dough.

6. Finally, stretch the dough by lightly picking up the rim and gently stretching it away from the centre. This will give you a consistent interior and a consistent pizza.

NOTE

All topping quantities are guidelines that will ensure your pizza doesn't feel underdressed, so to speak. You may like to use less (or perhaps more!). Try our suggested quantities and figure out what you like.

7. Dust your wooden peel with semolina and gently drag the pizza dough onto the peel. Apply your toppings (see opposite) now. At this point you can make any final adjustments to make sure the shape is even, the toppings are evenly applied and so on.

8. Use your pizza peel to slide the dough onto your preheated pizza stone. Bake for approximately 15–20 minutes. If you're using a Gozney or other pizza oven, slide it straight in; the cooking time will be much shorter (check your manual for the most accurate bake times).

FOUR-ONION PIZZA

⅓ cup (80 ml) garlic cream (page 224)

½ cup (50 g) three-cheese mix (page 224)

1 roasted whole brown onion (see fougasse recipe, page 67), sliced into rounds

½ red onion, sliced into thin rounds

½ cup (50 g) thinly sliced leek, washed thoroughly and dried

3 spring onions (scallions), cut into 2.5 cm (1 inch) lengths

Spread your base with garlic cream, leaving a 2 cm (¾ inch) border around the edge. Scatter the cheese mix evenly over the cream, followed by the roasted onion, red onion, leek and spring onion. Season with salt and pepper and bake.

SWEET-POTATO PIZZA

1 whole sweet potato

⅓ cup (80 ml) garlic cream (page 224)

½ cup (50 g) three-cheese mix (page 224)

60–100 g (2¼–3½ oz) feta, crumbled

¼ cup (45 g) pitted and roughly chopped Kalamata olives

1 small rosemary sprig, leaves picked

I like to roast sweet potatoes in their jackets and keep them whole until I'm about to use them, otherwise I find they get watery. Heat the oven to 220°C (425°F), place the sweet potato on a baking tray and roast for 45 minutes to 1 hour until very soft.

When you're ready to top the pizza, break off pieces of sweet potato that are of a similar size to the feta, using as much as your heart desires.

Spread your base with garlic cream, leaving a 2 cm (¾ inch) border around the edge. Scatter the cheese mix evenly over the cream, followed by the sweet potato, feta, olives and rosemary. Season with salt and pepper and bake.

PEPPERONI PIZZA

¼ cup (60 ml) rosso sauce (page 223)

½ cup (50 g) three-cheese mix (page 224)

1 ball fior di latte, torn up

100 g pepperoni, thinly sliced

Honey, to taste

The only way to make pepperoni pizza is to cover every inch of the dough with rounds of pepperoni. Anything less is too sparse and you'll forget what you're eating. Buy a whole sausage of the best available quality so you're not at risk of encountering this problem.

Spread your base with sauce, leaving a 2 cm (¾ inch) border. Scatter the cheese mix evenly over the top, followed by fior di latte and pepperoni slices. Bake, and once the pizza comes out of the oven, give it a generous drizzle of honey.

Everything Bagels

→ Tarte flambée → Pizzette → Bagel empanadas two ways
→ Mini bagel souvlakis

88–107

Our everything bagels

MAKES 10 BAGELS

The brilliant thing about this 'everything bagel' recipe is that the dough is also the basis of thin, crisp tarte flambée (or pizza for that matter), pizzette, empanadas and souvlaki. Who would have thought that bagels could give you all that?

This is a dough that keeps remarkably well, too. Make it when your starter is ready or you have some time up your sleeve and it will be waiting for you, good as new, in a few days' time for bagels. Or use it up to five days later for pizza or souvlaki. My advice is to always have some in your fridge. (It also makes a nice homemade gift!)

Despite the actual shaping of the bagels needing a bit of skill, the mixing is super easy and the resting period is short. Unlike all our other doughs, it's got a low hydration and contains commercial yeast.

You'll need to begin this recipe 17–18 hours before you want to eat.

BAKING INGREDIENTS AND PERCENTAGES		
Ripe starter (page 36)	150 g (5½ oz)	20%
Strong (baker's) flour	750 g (1 lb 10 oz)	100%
Filtered water, at 5–10°C (40–50°F)	390 g (13¾ oz)	52%
Old dough (see notes)	150 g (5½ oz)	20%
Barley (or rice) malt syrup	7 g (⅛ oz)	1%
Raw sugar	52 g (1¾ oz)	7%
Fine pink salt	18.5 g (¾ oz)	2.5%
Dried yeast (see note)	3 g (¹⁄₁₆ oz)	0.4%

My advice is to always have some of this dough in your fridge.

MIXING

EXTRA INGREDIENTS

Multi-seed mix
(page 222), sesame
seeds or poppyseeds,
for sprinkling

NOTES

If you don't have any
Nordic Ware proofing
trays with lids, simply
use baking trays and tea
towels to proof and bake.

You'll notice the water
temperature for bagels
is much colder than what
we use for our other
breads. That's because
we're not needing to
kickstart the natural
fermentation like in
a sourdough.

The old dough can be
any white dough that has
been in the fridge for less
than 5 days. Alternatively,
when you begin baking
from this book you can
also take some dough
from your first bread
trials with the country
loaf (see page 46).

For future bagel-making
fun, hold back some
of your bagel dough
whenever you bake and
store it in the fridge.
It's also important to
remember that old bagel
dough is one of the
highlights of this book:
it's your ticket to pizza,
flatbread and more!

We use only a tiny amount
of dried yeast in these,
because it's so powerful.

1. You have two choices when mixing the bagel dough: mix it in your stainless steel bowl (as with the country loaf recipe on page 46) or use a stand mixer with the dough hook attachment; normally stand mixers don't suit our bread, but this dough is a lower hydration, so you can get away with it here.

2. Follow the directions to prep your starter in the country loaf recipe on page 46, then measure out all your ingredients. Add the wet ingredients – that is the starter, water, old dough and malt syrup – to the bowl, then add the dry ingredients – the flour, sugar, salt and yeast – and begin to mix.

3. If mixing by hand, then you need to work vigorously and make sure that the ingredients are fully combined and developed well. In the bowl, start mixing from the outside and work your way in as you rotate the bowl. Continue mixing until it's shaggy. The hydration of this dough will mean that everything will combine quickly, but it can't be developed by folding – you have to knead. Tip the dough onto an unfloured bench (this dough is less sticky than others) and knead for 10 minutes. Use your pastry scraper to bring the dough back towards you and keep your other hand as your 'dough hand'.

   If you're using a stand mixer, fit it with the dough hook attachment and begin mixing on a moderate speed before quickly shifting it up to high. Mix for approximately 10 minutes.

4. Once the dough is mixed, it should feel somewhere between pasta dough and bread: smooth to the touch with no dry remnants of ingredients. Rest it for 10 minutes, covered with a pizza tray or a clean tea towel, in an ambient spot. At this point you could also use this dough to make pizzette (page 100), or refrigerate it for a day or more and make flatbreads (page 106).

SHAPING

1. Prepare a clean bench for shaping the bagels, allowing plenty of room for rolling and shaping. If you're not ready to bake yet, place the dough in an oiled, sealed container in your refrigerator. It'll keep for up to 5 days at this point (or 3 months frozen) and can be used for any of the recipes in this chapter. If it's frozen, make sure to thaw it first.

2. When you're ready to bake, tip the rested dough onto your cleaned, unfloured bench and shape it into a flat rectangle with your hands (images 01–02). Make the edges as straight and flat as you can. This is your bagel slab. It should be about 5 cm (2 inches) high and as even in height as possible.

3. Now that you have your slab on the bench, grab your dough scraper and start scoring rows (that is, running from left to right) into the dough, 3 cm (1¼ inches) apart (image 03). You want between 10 and 11 rows. This is where you will cut your strips of dough that end up being the bagels.

4. Cut the first strip with your dough scraper then pull it away from your slab (image 04). Roll this strip on the bench so it's smooth and even and measures approximately 25 cm (10 inches) long. It should look like a giant sausage or ribbon of dough.

5. Loop the dough strip around your hand and into your palm, arranging it so the ends of the strip meet in your palm near where your thumb and index finger join (image 05). Leaving about 3 cm (1¼ inches) overlapping, tear the excess dough away and place it on the bench (pieces of scrap dough can be joined together and refrigerated to be used for other recipes in this chapter, or anything that calls for old dough).

6. You now have the bagel strip in your hand and you just need to seal the ends. With the bagel's join in your palm being held by your thumb and index finger, drop your hand to the bench and apply pressure against the bench to seal, rolling the dough backwards and forwards until it's joined (image 06).

7. Repeat the process with the remaining strips from your bagel slab (image 07).

8. Once all the bagels are shaped, we recommend sprinkling them with our multi-seed mix (page 222). To do this, prepare a large bowl of cold water at 10°C (50°F) or below, a tea towel, and a tray filled with the seed mix. Dunk each bagel into the water (image 08) and then shake off the excess over the cloth. Place the bagel into the seed mix, toss it and make sure that the seeds completely cover the bagel all over (image 09).

9. Once all the bagels are shaped (and covered with seeds, if you like), lay them in a Nordic Ware proofing tray (with a lid) lined with baking paper. You should be able to fit four or five bagels before moving to a second tray. Cover with the lid of the proofing tray and place at the bottom of the fridge (where your crisper lives) to proof for at least 8 hours and up to 12 hours. Alternatively, you can bake the same day as shaping by covering the tray and proofing the bagels at room temperature for 3–4 hours.

→

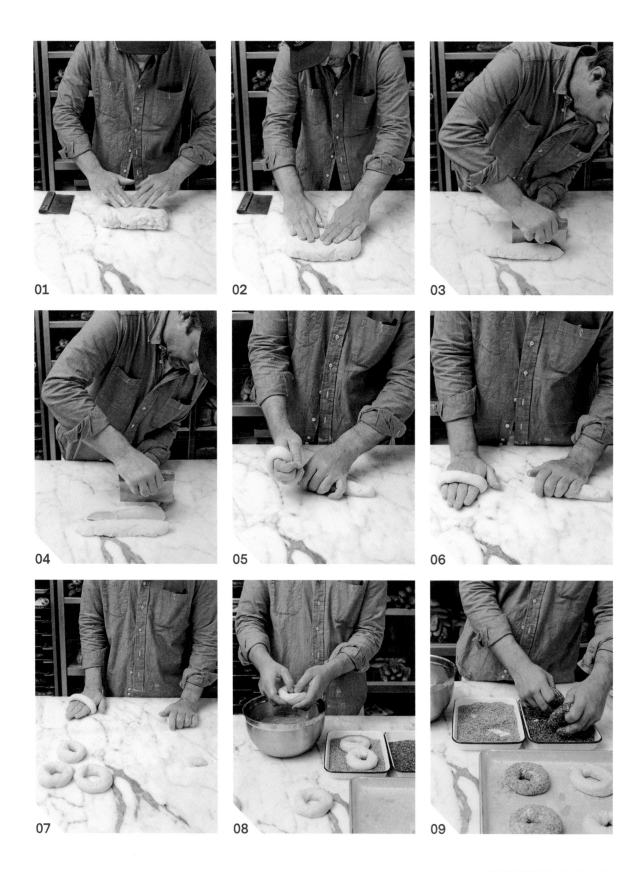

BAKING

1. Take the bagels from the fridge approximately 3 hours ahead of bake time and place them in a warm area of your house. If you've rested them at room temperature, skip this step.

2. An hour before baking, heat the oven to 250°C (480°F), or as high as it will go. Before you turn it on, make sure your oven is set up with two racks or shelves. You will need the top shelf for your bagels and the one underneath for a tray of water, which will create steam.

3. When the oven has come to temperature and is ready to bake, uncover one of your bagel trays. Fill a second tray with higher edges with 300 ml (10½ fl oz) water.

4. Place the bagel tray on the top shelf and the water tray on the bottom, and bake for 30 minutes until the bagels are doubled in size and have a deep golden brown crust.

5. Once the bagels are ready, remove them from the oven and transfer to a wire cooling rack. Let them cool for at least 10 minutes before slicing, or keep them in a cloth or paper bag. Bagels toast well, freeze well and are great turned into chips (see page 215), too.

6. Repeat the baking process for the second tray of bagels.

Lo-fi launch

When I found a site to open our little bakery, it seemed perfect. It had parking out front, lots of schools nearby, a café next door where people could get coffee. Even better, it came with three-phase power and a food permit in place, two headaches no new business owner wants to deal with.

It also came with warnings from every other shop on the street that the site was cursed.

That was literally the word people used. They all shared the same landlord. Some of them even had restraining orders against her.

But I knew that this neighbourhood was home to a community that appreciated good food and would also inspire me.

I met the landlord, weighed up the positives and negatives, and went for it. It was plug-and-play. We didn't have the money to do it any other way.

We put a wooden board over the kitchen sink and used it as a bench for the loaves we loaded into the oven. We couldn't afford signage, so we just painted the words 'Baker Bleu' on a wooden baking peel and propped it out the front on the pavement.

It was seriously DIY.

We opened with just three products: two-kilogram country loaves, bagels and baguettes. When people suggested that we do pastries or sandwiches or coffee, I was adamant: bread was what we were about.

I wanted Baker Bleu pared back to the product. We wanted to highlight that we were doing something that other bakeries in Melbourne weren't: cold-fermented loaves, baked in the morning, which enticed people with that distinctive fresh-bread aroma.

There are businesses that open and they're polished from day dot. They've got a whole team behind them, marketing them, making decisions about what they should sell to bring in more people, and so on.

Some of these are great businesses. But they haven't had that journey of finding out who they are and what they are about. There's so much magic in that process.

That said, we now offer much more than just three types of bread. But having the freshest product possible has dictated our decisions.

We don't do a whole range of pies or a huge range of sandwiches or whatever. The product's

We opened with just three products: two-kilogram country loaves, bagels and baguettes.

integrity is king. That has led us down certain paths and not in other directions.

We've also learned a lot by listening to our customers. We wouldn't have our challah loaf if we hadn't taken their feedback on board.

About four years in, Mia realised that we were working so hard and investing so much in the process of making the bread, that we were neglecting other things. She was getting sick all the time. We were both worse for wear mentally. And we had hardly put any money into marketing or the way our shops looked.

Opening our pastry production bakery in Hawksburn was a turning point. This was the first shop that we didn't build ourselves, or fit out by begging and borrowing materials from friends, neighbours or family. We hired an architect who had designed some of Melbourne's top restaurants.

Now, with Baker Bleu in Double Bay, we have two beautiful bakeries with striking interiors that look totally different to other bakeries.

Baker Bleu might have been my idea, but we'd still be a microbakery today if it wasn't for Mia's business expertise and her family, who dropped everything to help us build not one but two bakeries. That injection of blood, sweat and tears? You can't get a bigger leg-up than that when you start a business.

At the start of Baker Bleu I thought, 'I've got no idea what I'm doing. We're just going to start off making bagels and a two-kilo loaf.' I envisioned the product on the shelf, how it should look and taste. But everything after that has been a surprise.

I have no sentimentality about our shoebox of a first shop. But I am glad that we stuck to our guns and grew the business the way we wanted to.

And we've still got the board – it sits on display, a little worse for wear, at our Caulfield North shop.

Tarte flambée

MAKES 2 TARTES

This is basically France's answer to pizza. It's thin and crisp, sharp in flavour and cheesy. It's the perfect snack with a glass of riesling or beer. Note that it's best eaten when it's quite hot, because it's an unleavened dough with a crunchy texture.

Because the dough does not need to be leavened, old bagel dough left over from your bagel adventures is perfect as a base. You could try to use fresh dough, but you'll get a more doughy result, and then can you really call it tarte flambée?

INGREDIENTS

400 g (14 oz) old bagel dough (page 90; up to 5 days old, thawed if frozen)

1 tablespoon sunflower oil

250 g (9 oz) crème fraîche

250 g (9 oz) three-cheese mix (page 224)

1 whole nutmeg

180 g (6½ oz) smoked bacon lardons (shop-bought is fine)

1 bunch of spring onions (scallions), green tops sliced

1. Heat the oven to 250°C (480°F), or as high as it will go. Remove the bagel dough from the fridge.

2. On a lightly floured bench, divide the bagel dough in half. Cover one half with a tea towel and roll out the other half on the bench with a rolling pin (or wine bottle) to a rectangular shape, rolling it as thinly as possible (this will give it the crisp texture you want). Don't forget to rotate the dough to get an even result.

3. Grease a pizza or baking tray with sunflower oil, just to coat it with a thin film. Lay your dough on the tray and gently stretch it so it covers as much of the tray as possible and there are no folded bits.

4. Spoon half of the crème fraîche onto the dough and spread it using either the back of a spoon or a pastry brush. It needs to be evenly spread.

5. Sprinkle half the cheese mix onto the crème fraîche, evenly covering the surface. Grate over half the nutmeg and season generously with sea salt and freshly ground pepper.

6. Sprinkle half the lardons and spring onions over the top, then season once again with salt and pepper. Bake for 15–20 minutes until the base is crisp and the top is a beautiful combination of crunchy lardons and melted cheese. Repeat with the second portion of dough.

7. Remove from the oven and, while it's hot, cut it into approximately eight coaster-sized squares to serve.

Pizzette

MAKES 25 (APPROXIMATELY 6 CM/2½ INCHES IN DIAMETER)

The dough that doesn't quit, our bagel dough, again shines here in a neat little aperitivo snack. The salty, cheesy contrast of these small pizzas with a bitter drink, like a Negroni (or even a Negroni Sbagliato) is super delicious.

Unlike our pizza recipe, which uses a ciabatta dough, these have more chew and softness, a bit like a pita. Top them with ham, roasted capsicum (pepper), torn mozzarella or anything else your heart desires.

A quick note on quantities: using a full quantity of bagel dough will give you up to 50 pizzette. If you want to make 50, go for it. It will be a pizza party – and pizza is, after all, a party food. We suggest using half the bagel dough and keeping the remainder in the fridge for another use.

INGREDIENTS

½ quantity bagel dough (page 90)
1 quantity rosso sauce (page 223)
1 tin Ortiz anchovies, drained, plus extra as needed
25 Manzanilla olives, halved and pitted, plus extra as needed
1 quantity three-cheese mix (page 224)

1. Follow steps 1 to 4 of the bagel recipe, up until you rest the dough. If you've made the dough the same day, rest it for 10 minutes at room temperature; if you made it earlier, remove it from the fridge and leave it at room temperature for 10 minutes.

2. Tip the rested dough onto a clean, unfloured bench with plenty of space. Shape the dough into a flat rectangle with your hands, about 5 cm (2 inches) high and as even in height as possible.

3. With your dough scraper, cut strips off the slab about a quarter of the width of your scraper. From each strip, cut and weigh 30 g (1 oz) pieces of dough and shape them into balls.

4. Once you have all the pizzette cut and shaped, place them neatly onto a proofing tray lined with baking paper, lifting them off the bench with your dough scraper. Cover with a lid or a tea towel and set aside.

5. Place a non-stick baking tray in the oven and heat the oven to 250°C (480°F). If your tray isn't non-stick, line it with baking paper

6. Arrange your prepared toppings within easy reach of where you'll place the hot tray to assemble the pizzette.

7. Flatten out the pizzette balls between your palms – you want them quite thin and approximately 7 cm (2¾ inches) in diameter – and place them back in the proofing tray.

8. When the oven has reached 250°C (480°F), place a heat mat or similar on your bench and place the preheated pizza tray on top.

9. Transfer the flattened pizzette to the tray (about 8–10 per tray) and, working quickly, top them with 2 teaspoons of rosso sauce, a whole anchovy or an olive (or both), then 2 teaspoons of cheese mix.

10. Bake for 10 minutes, remove and admire your 'bonita' pizzette before serving them to your guests. Repeat with remaining dough and toppings.

Bagel empanadas two ways

An empanada is a great pre-dinner snack or a meal on its own alongside a leafy salad. Typically, the dough is made with flour, water, salt and fat (traditionally lard), but our bagel dough lends itself really well to empanadas. They will be slightly less flaky, more like the texture of a pizza, but it's cool to have yet another thing to do with your old bagel dough.

You will get better results using bagel dough that's been in the fridge for a few days. The dough will be low in activity and won't go too crazy on the leavening.

BEEF AND OLIVE EMPANADAS

MAKES 12

INGREDIENTS

3 eggs

⅓ cup (55 g) pitted and roughly chopped Manzanilla or Kalamata olives

100 g (3½ oz) lightly salted butter

2 large onions, quartered then thinly sliced into crescents

1 tablespoon dried chilli flakes

1 tablespoon ground cumin

1 tablespoon smoked paprika

5 spring onions (scallions), whites and greens kept separate and very finely chopped

2 tablespoons extra-virgin olive oil

450 g (1 lb) well-marbled beef, such as sirloin or tri-tip, roughly diced into 2 cm (¾ inch) pieces

2 tablespoons oregano (dried or fresh), finely chopped if fresh

480 g (1 lb 1 oz) old bagel dough (page 90; up to 5 days old, thawed if frozen)

Eggwash, for brushing

1. Bring a saucepan of water to the boil, add the eggs, then lower the heat to medium and boil gently for 9 minutes. Drain, then peel the eggs under cold running water and allow to cool.

2. Roughly chop the eggs into small pieces, and toss in a small bowl with the chopped olives.

3. Melt the butter in a large frying pan over low heat. Add the onions and cook, stirring frequently to avoid them burning, until translucent, about 8–10 minutes.

4. Add the chilli flakes, cumin, paprika and the white part of the spring onions to the pan and fry for another 3–5 minutes, stirring, until the spring onion is softened. Stir in the green part of the spring onions, season to taste with sea salt and freshly ground pepper and transfer to a bowl.

5. Return the pan to medium heat, add the olive oil and then the beef, in batches if necessary. Cook, stirring occasionally, until browned all over, about 3 minutes; remember you're going to bake it afterwards so you don't want to overcook it.

6. Remove the pan from the heat, stir in the onion mixture and the oregano and leave to cool.

7. Heat the oven to 180°C (350°F). Remove the bagel dough from the fridge and lightly flour a bench in a spot with plenty of space to work. Roll out the dough into a long rectangle as thin as possible (about 3 mm/⅛ inch) and about 10 cm (4 inches) wide, adding more flour if necessary to prevent sticking; it should be thin but not translucent.

8. Place heaped tablespoons or so of the beef mix along the length of the dough at 3 cm (1¼ inch) intervals, leaving an even border, approximately 5 cm (2 inches), above and below.

9. Place a teaspoon or so of egg and olive mix on top of the beef mix.

10. With a small pastry brush, brush a small amount of water along the top edge of the dough, about 2 cm (¾ inch) wide. This will assist in sealing.

11. Begin to fold the bottom length of the dough over the mounds of empanada filling, a bit like making ravioli, then seal against the damp edge at the top by pressing down with your fingers. Once it's sealed the whole way along, use the side of your hand to gently depress the spaces between the mounds of filling. Once each parcel is clearly defined, separate them with a small, sharp knife, slicing down the centre of the gap between each parcel, then trimming the edges to form half-moons.

12. To seal the parcels, press the tip of a fork around the open edges to give a crinkled finish, ensuring you seal them well, otherwise they may pop open.

13. Place the empanadas on baking trays lined with baking paper, allowing four to five per tray. Glaze with eggwash if you'd like a shiny finish, then bake for 15–17 minutes until golden.

14. Remove from the oven, allow to cool for 10 minutes or so, then serve.

→

VEGETARIAN EMPANADAS

INGREDIENTS

Refer to the recipe on page 103, replacing the beef with 2 sweet potatoes and the eggs with a jar (320 g/11¼ oz) of marinated feta.

1. Heat the oven to 180°C (350°F). Peel the sweet potatoes and cut into 2 cm (¾ inch) dice. Lightly toss in olive oil, then spread on baking trays (you will need at least two) and roast for 30 minutes or until tender.

2. Skip to steps 3–4 of the beef and olive empanadas recipe (page 103), leaving everything in the pan, then skip to step 6 and combine the roasted sweet potato and oregano with the onion mixture in the pan.

3. Move to steps 7 and 8, then top the vegetarian empanada mix with half a crumbled feta cube and a teaspoon or so of chopped olives.

4. Proceed with the folding, sealing and baking as directed; cool briefly, then serve.

Yet another cool thing to do with your old bagel dough.

Mini bagel souvlakis

MAKES 30

The bagel dough once again lends itself to another super-easy application: pita for use in lamb souvlaki, or anything that you would like to wrap into a charred, chewy flatbread.

By forming the bagel dough into small discs that we place on a hot grill, it turns into a super-moreish flatbread with smoky char that's the perfect vessel for slow-roasted lamb and accompaniments. I've suggested salted cucumber, pickled onions and toum, but feel free to take this in your own direction.

The lamb shoulder will obviously feed many and fill loads of mini souvlaki, so preparing a larger batch of bagel dough (see page 90) than usual isn't a bad idea.

INGREDIENTS

Old bagel dough
    (1–7 days old;
    see page 90), 40 g
    (1½ oz) per serve

Lamb

2.5 kg (5 lb 8 oz) whole
    bone-in lamb shoulder
6 garlic cloves, peeled
¼ cup (35 g) sea
    salt flakes
¼ cup (7 g) oregano
    leaves, finely chopped
1 tablespoon
    sweet paprika
1 tablespoon
    ground cumin
2 lemons, peeled then
    chopped finely (juice
    1 before chopping;
    you'll need the juice for
    the salted cucumbers)
¼ cup (60 ml) olive oil
200 ml (7 fl oz)
    filtered water

Salted cucumbers

3 Lebanese cucumbers
Large pinch of sea salt
Juice of 1 lemon
1 small bunch of dill,
    finely chopped

1. To prepare the lamb, place the shoulder in a heavy, deep roasting tray, preferably one that fits in the fridge. Or use a large container or bowl.

2. Place a chopping board on a tea towel or damp cloth to secure it. Slice the garlic thinly, then sprinkle a little of the sea salt over it. Now, use the tip of your knife to press the garlic slices down against the chopping board, almost mashing them with the salt to create a garlic paste. Place this in a small bowl, add the oregano, paprika, cumin, lemon, olive oil, remaining salt and a liberal grind of black pepper and combine well.

3. Spread this marinade all over the lamb shoulder, covering the meat completely and massaging it in well. Cover with plastic wrap, and refrigerate overnight, or for at least 3 hours at room temperature, to marinate.

4. Heat the oven to 150°C (300°F). If you marinated the lamb in the fridge overnight, allow it to come to room temperature for approximately 1 hour. Pour the filtered water into the tray, then roast the lamb for 6–7 hours or until the meat is very, very tender.

5. Remove lamb from the oven and rest for 20–40 minutes. After 40 minutes, it should be cool enough to shred into small chunks with a fork or two.

6. While the lamb is resting, prepare your salted cucumbers and quick-pickled onions. For the cucumbers, slice them thinly, then place them in a bowl and season with the salt. Add the lemon juice and dill and combine well.

7. After the cucumbers have pickled for 5 minutes, remove the bagel dough from the fridge and weigh out the total quantity you will need for your desired number of pita breads.

8. Lightly flour the bench, then roll your bagel dough into a log. With a sharp knife or pastry card, cut this log into discs weighing approximately 40 g (1½ oz) each.

9. Pick up each disc and flatten it between your palms. You want something that is roughly the size of a drink coaster and about 3 mm (⅛ inch) in thickness. Making them thin is fine because they'll puff up.

Quick-pickled onions
(page 223), to serve
Jar of toum (bought),
to serve

10. Heat a chargrill pan (or the grill plate of your barbecue) to high. Once the pan is scorching hot, grill each pita for a maximum of 2 minutes a side. Use a steel spatula to lift the pita off the grill and turn it. They won't puff as much as naan but they will puff slightly. You'll know they're ready when they get firmer around the edges. Cover them with a tea towel to keep warm.

11. When you're ready to serve, place a pita on a serving dish, spread it with a tablespoon of toum and top it with shredded lamb, followed by some cucumber and pickled onion. You won't be able to wrap these mini souvlakis – they are more like a three- or four-bite souvlaki tapa.

Dark rye tin loaf

MAKES 2 x 750 G (1 LB 10 OZ) LOAVES

SPECIAL EQUIPMENT

2 loaf tins, at 13 x 24 cm
(5 x 9½ inches)

This recipe was inspired by Mia's travels to Sweden, where she fell in love with the heavier style of bread eaten there. At the bakery, we were looking to introduce a bread like that with deep flavour. By chance, we had also met the owners of Brick Lane Brewing, a Melbourne craft brewery that had just opened a new facility.

They wanted to collaborate and we wanted to try making a rye bread entirely with brewer's wort to achieve the big complex flavour we were striving for.

Wort is the beginning stage of the brewing process – it's almost like a tea brewed out of the grains used to make beer. All that sugar and moisture leads to insane amounts of flavour. While we don't expect you to get your hands on brewer's wort, this recipe does call for beer. And my suggestion is, the darker, the better.

This dough is super hydrated, almost like a cake batter. We use non-stick loaf tins and allow the dough to sit overnight after baking. It's so hydrated it almost needs to cure overnight.

Enjoy this loaf the way some of our wholesale customers use it: with super-oily fish, anything sharp in flavour, or with something rich like gribiche, crème fraîche or labne. It's also a fantastic loaf for schmears.

Begin this recipe 2 days before you want to serve.

BAKING INGREDIENTS AND PERCENTAGES		
Ripe starter (page 36)	160 g (5¾ oz)	30%
Whole rye stoneground flour	530 g (1 lb 3 oz)	100%
Water, at about 10°C (50°F)	320 g (11¼ oz)	60%
Ale or dark beer (such as stout)	320 g (11¼ oz)	60%
Pink salt	13.5 g (½ oz)	2.5%

EXTRA INGREDIENTS

1 batch seeded spelt
mix (page 222),
for sprinkling

1. Follow the directions to prep your starter in the country loaf recipe on page 46. Measure out all the ingredients and add the flour and salt to a large bowl (image 01, page 111). Add the ripe starter (images 02–03), keeping it away from the salt, then add the water, followed by the ale (image 04). Add all but 2 tablespoons of seed mix.

2. Because this dough is so hydrated, we are going to mix it with a spatula or pastry card. Start mixing from the inside in a circular motion, gradually moving outwards.

→

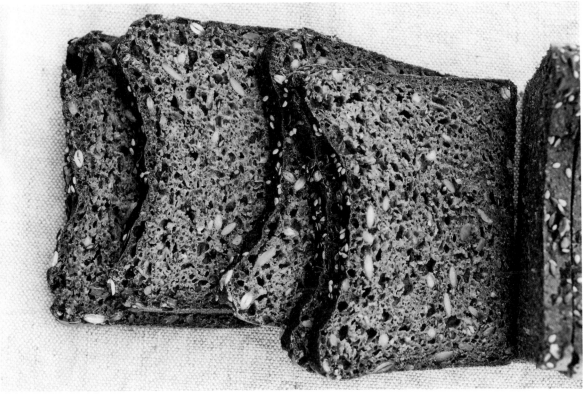

3. Once you've formed a dough (it will look like cake batter; image 05), continue mixing for 10 minutes to allow it to develop. Continually scrape down the sides of the bowl to ensure all ingredients are thoroughly incorporated (image 06).

4. After 10 minutes, take a large jug and fill it two-thirds to the top with water. Have your loaf tins, pastry card and kitchen scales within easy reach.

5. Place one loaf tin on the scale and tare the scale so the weight reads zero. Dip the pastry card or one hand into the jug of water (this will prevent the dough from sticking) and use it to scrape out some of the dough into the tin (image 07). You want to fill the tin with 600 g (1 lb 5 oz) of dough (image 08). Once you've got the correct amount of dough in the tin, use your spatula or pastry card to flatten and smooth the top. Repeat to fill a second tin with the remaining dough.

6. Sprinkle the reserved seed mix evenly over the top of the loaves (image 09). Pat the seeds down a little so they're incorporated slightly into the dough.

7. Rest the dough in the loaf tins overnight (at least 12 hours) in the bottom of your fridge (where the crisper lives). There's no need to cover the dough because the seed mix protects it.

8. Remove the tins the next day and leave at ambient temperature for 3–4 hours to finish proofing. (Alternatively, you could leave one loaf in the fridge longer, and bake it the next day.)

9. In the final hour of the dough coming to room temperature, heat the oven to 220°C (425°F). Bake the loaves for an hour, then turn the oven off and leave in the oven for another hour.

10. Remove the loaves from the tins and place on a wire cooling rack overnight, upside down, with the bottom of the loaves facing up. This will allow the dough to cure. If you skip this step, the bread will taste like unbaked cake.

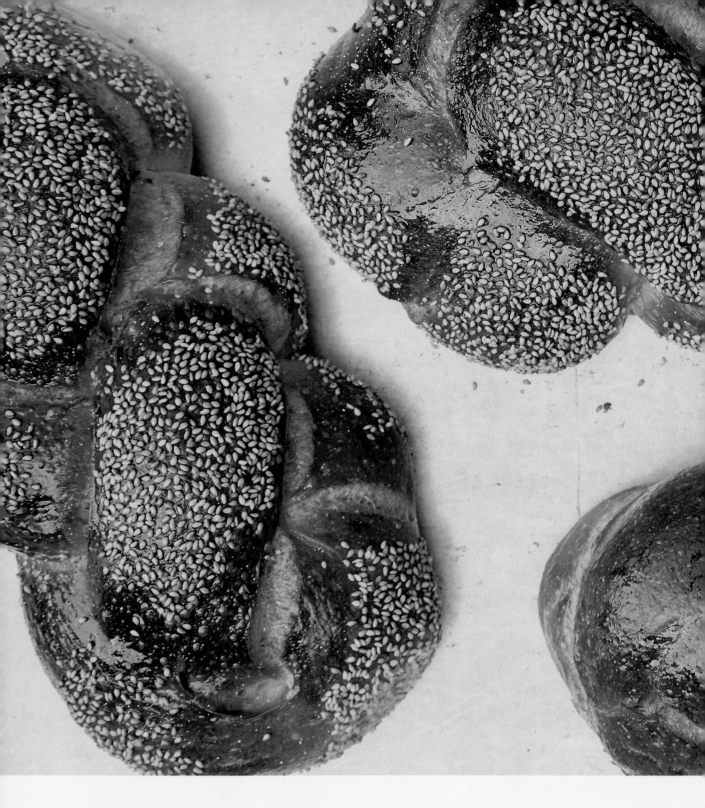

Challah

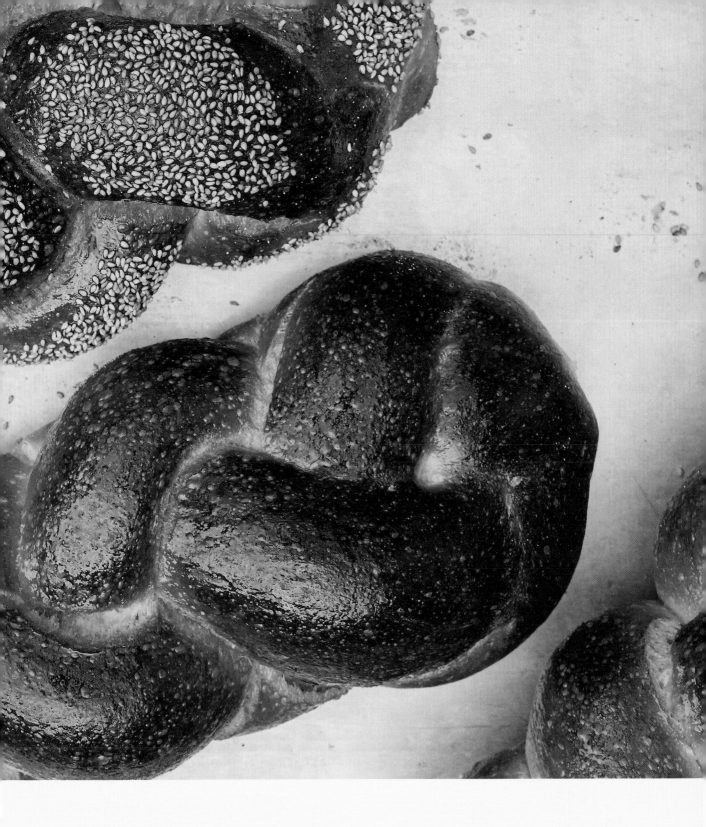

→ Round challah → Coffee, walnut and cinnamon morning
buns → Challah buns → Tin loaf (for your perfect sausage sanga)

Challah

MAKES 2 x 600 G (1 LB 5 OZ) CHALLAH LOAVES

Opening a bakery in Elsternwick, one of the centres of Jewish life in Melbourne, I suppose it was inevitable that we'd end up selling challah. But it wasn't something that crossed our minds initially. For one thing, we weren't allowed to cook with eggs under our existing food permit. Mia and I are also gentiles. Was it right for us to make challah?

But after three months or so, when people started coming in to see what this new Elsternwick bakery was all about, the questions about challah came thick and fast. Everyone was an expert, too. They were full of tips on ingredients, how we should shape it, what the texture should be like. It seemed like challah was in our future.

To get around the egg thing, I decided to combine a few doughs I'd done before and use things that we already had lying around.

Mia has been obsessed with oat milk for the last decade, so we always have that on hand. Sunflower oil is used to grease our dough tubs at the bakery. We were making granola in the bakery already so we had maple syrup.

The result – a cross between our ciabatta dough and a really hydrated version of our bagel recipe – is a texture like a milk bun and a super-glossy finish. The sugar content in our bagel is close to being on a par with where it should be in a challah. The whole thing is vegan and, most importantly, it's kosher.

A challah with no eggs stumped a few people at first, especially because we'd found a glaze that looked just like eggwash. The community, however, came to appreciate having a challah made locally that was sourdough-based and easier to digest than many other challahs out there.

Take it to someone's house to break bread at the start of a meal, or use it for a fantastic chicken schnitzel sandwich. This dough is also the starting point for the other recipes in this chapter, like flavoured challah, round challah, morning buns, challah buns and a tin loaf perfect for sangas.

→

BAKING INGREDIENTS AND PERCENTAGES		
Ripe starter (page 36)	105 g (3½ oz)	20%
Old dough (see note)	105 g (3½ oz)	20%
Strong (baker's) flour	520 g (1 lb 2 oz)	100%
Oat milk, at 28°C (82°F) or room temperature	365 g (12¾ oz)	70%
Sunflower oil	45 g (1¾ oz)	9%
Barley (or rice) malt syrup	5 g (⅛ oz)	1%
Raw sugar	30 g (1 oz)	6%
Fine pink salt	13 g (½ oz)	2.5%
Dried yeast	2 g (¹⁄₁₆ oz)	0.5%

EXTRA INGREDIENTS

Sunflower oil,
for greasing
1 tablespoon oat milk
or water, for glazing
Sesame seeds,
poppyseeds or the
multi-seed mix on
page 222 (optional),
for sprinkling
Maple glaze (page 225),
for brushing

NOTE

You can use old bagel
dough or old country-
loaf dough that has been
stored in the fridge. In
either case, it should be
no more than a week old.

1. Follow the directions to prep your starter in the country loaf recipe on page 46, then follow the country loaf mixing method up to the end of step 6, but using the ingredients above, adding the oat milk in place of the water, the oil with the malt syrup, then the sugar, salt and yeast at the end.

2. Once you've formed the dough and have no loose bits remaining around the edge of the bowl, use a little extra sunflower oil to grease the sides of the bowl. Give the dough one more dumpling fold, then cover the bowl with a tea towel or pizza tray to allow the dough to bulk rest in a warm place for an hour.

3. After an hour, remove the cover to give the dough another dumpling fold. Leave to ferment, covered, for a further hour. At this point, you can keep going, or you can skip to page 122 to make round challah, page 124 to make morning buns, page 127 to make challah buns or page 128 to make tin loaf.

4. Tip the dough onto a floured surface and divide it into four 300 g (10½ oz) rectangles with your pastry card.

5. You want to create small logs (or mini baguettes) out of your dough before you roll them out, then braid them into a long challah. To do so, lay each rectangle in front of you with the long edge parallel to you. Working from the top of the rectangle, fold a third of the dough down towards the centre (image 01). Repeat this step from the bottom, making sure you fold over the top and seal it against itself. The trick is not dusting with too much flour; if you are excessive on the flour, it won't stick. If it can't stick then there will be no tension in the dough and it won't hold its shape. Once you've shaped all four pieces, allow them to rest for 5 minutes.

6. Now, with your hands flat out and extended, use the bottom part of your palms to roll the dough upwards, away from you, then downwards, towards you, applying pressure to make the challah dough longer. By the time you've finished rolling the dough, each piece should resemble a long sausage, and be more than 4 large hand widths long (image 02).

7. To braid your first challah, lay two lengths of dough across each other on a lightly floured surface so they form an X shape (image 03). If you're right handed, the bottom piece of dough should run from the top right to bottom left. If you're left handed, lay the pieces the opposite way.

→

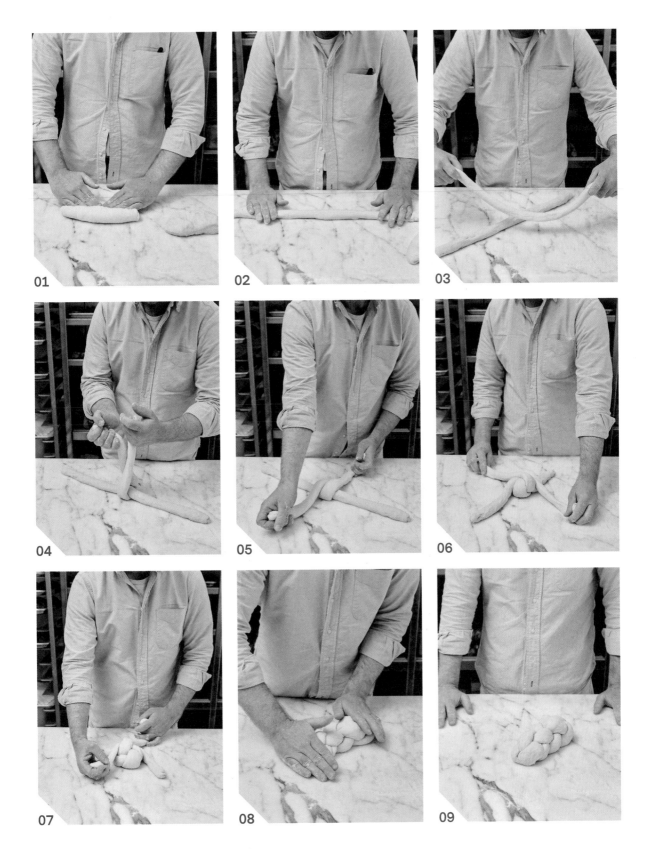

8. Lift up each end of the bottom piece of dough (image 04). The end closest to you should be in your right hand and the top end in your left hand if you're following the right-hand method. Cross the top piece over the bottom piece (image 05), followed by bottom over top (image 06), and repeat this until you have no more dough to braid, tucking any excess under and pressing it together gently (images 07–09).

9. Transfer the challah to a baking tray lined with baking paper and cover with a tea towel.

10. Repeat the process with the remaining two lengths of dough to create a second challah.

11. Proof the challahs for 40 minutes to 1 hour at room temperature until billowy and at least doubled in size.

12. While they are proofing, heat the oven to 250°C (480°F). When they're ready to bake, brush the challah with oat milk or water; this helps to keep the loaf moist, creates steam and helps the seed mix stick (if you're using any). Once completely covered in glaze, cover with your chosen seeds, or leave as is.

13. Bake for 30 minutes or until golden. Remove from the oven and cool on a wire cooling rack for 5 minutes. Glaze with the maple glaze, covering the top of the challah entirely. As soon as the glaze is on, the challah is ready.

NOTE

Flame raisins are red in colour and larger than a sultana. They're super sweet and firm, which is why we like them. If you can't find them, substitute any raisin.

VARIATION

To make **raisin and cinnamon challah**, follow the challah dough recipe, but when you're weighing your dry ingredients, include 130 g (4¾ oz) whole flame raisins (see note) and 5 g (⅛ oz) ground cinnamon. Follow the remaining steps, then, prepare yourself for next-level sweetness and aroma while your challah bakes. This is fantastic eaten fresh but toasting it or using it for pain perdu takes it to another dimension. And it's still vegan!

Round challah

MAKES 2 X 600 G (1 LB 5 OZ) LOAVES

Round challah is not only very beautiful, it's the traditional shape to serve for Rosh Hashanah (or Jewish New Year). It symbolises the cycle of life.

We make ours into a spiral shape, rather than a round braid, which is much easier to do at home. Scatter yours with poppyseeds if you'd like to be super traditional.

INGREDIENTS

1 quantity of challah dough (page 114)
1 tablespoon oat milk or water, for glazing
Poppyseeds (optional), for sprinkling
Maple glaze (page 225), for brushing

1. Follow the core challah recipe (page 114) up until the end of step 3, when you're about to divide the dough. At the end of the bulk rise, you should have a dough that is billowy and has doubled in volume.

2. Now, instead of dividing the dough into four pieces, divide the dough into two 600 g (1 lb 5 oz) pieces with your pastry card.

3. With your hands, flatten each piece of dough into an even rectangle, approximately 2 cm (¾ inch) thick. With the widest part of the rectangle facing you, press down on the bottom part of the dough to anchor it, then take the top third of the rectangle and fold it towards the middle, then fold the bottom third into the middle to create a log. This is your pre-shape. Cover, and repeat with the other piece of dough. Rest the dough, covered, for up to 30 minutes at room temperature.

4. Lightly flour a bench, then transfer one of the dough logs onto it. Flatten the log into a rectangle again, then repeat the same folding process as before.

5. Once you have your new log, lengthen it by picking up the ends of the log and gently easing them away from the bench. Holding the dough, make a couple of small flapping motions with your hands. This will elongate the whole piece of dough naturally and effortlessly.

6. Now that you have achieved some more length in the dough, put the ends down. Lightly flour your hands and place both palms on the centre of the dough and roll your hands back and forth along the length of dough. Repeat this a couple of times, always starting from the centre, until you achieve the length of approximately 60 cm (24 inches). Be careful not to tear the dough or overwork it. If the dough is tight or starts to tear, give it a momentary rest.

7. Once the dough is the required length, it's time to spiral it. Take one end of the log and loosely curl it on itself, then continue to wind the dough around itself. Once you reach the end, tuck the tail underneath the spiral to secure it. Transfer the challah to a baking tray lined with baking paper and cover with a tea towel. Repeat the process for the second piece of dough.

8. Follow steps 11–12 of the core challah recipe to proof and glaze the dough, and heat the oven to 250°C (480°F).

9. Bake for 20 minutes or until golden. Remove from the oven and transfer to a wire cooling rack for 5 minutes to cool. Glaze the loaves with the maple glaze, covering the tops entirely. As soon as the glaze is on, they're ready to eat.

Coffee, walnut and cinnamon morning buns

MAKES 24

The beauty of the challah dough is its flexibility. You can make sweet challahs, use it for burger buns or, as in this instance, turn it into morning buns. All the folds and layers here catch the flavours of cinnamon and coffee, as well as creating lots of different textures in each bite.

The quantities in the core challah recipe will give you two batches of morning buns. You can go ahead and make both if you're feeding a crowd, or store half the dough in the freezer for another day, ready to thaw and then bake all on the same day.

INGREDIENTS

1 quantity of challah
    dough (page 114)
200 g (7 oz) activated
    walnuts, crushed
    (see note)
10 g (¼ oz) ground
    coffee beans
Maple glaze (page 225),
    for brushing

Cinnamon butter

300 g (10½ oz)
    brown sugar
20 g (¾ oz) ground
    cinnamon
Pinch of fine sea salt
250 g (9 oz) unsalted
    butter, at room
    temperature

1. Follow the core challah recipe (page 114) up until the end of step 3, when you're about to divide the dough. At the end of the bulk rise, you should have a dough that is billowy and has doubled in volume.

2. Meanwhile, while the dough is resting, make the cinnamon butter. In a stand mixer fitted with the paddle attachment, mix the sugar, cinnamon and salt together on low speed until well combined. Remove 2 tablespoons of this mix and set it aside. Now add the butter to the mixer, increase the speed to medium, and mix for 1–2 minutes until a thick, pale paste forms.

3. After the dough has finished resting, tip it onto a lightly floured surface and divide it into two 600 g (1 lb 5 oz) pieces with your pastry card.

4. Take one piece of dough and roll it out to a rectangle, roughly 25 x 35 cm (10 x 14 inches). Spread half the cinnamon butter on top as evenly as possible, going all the way to the edges, then sprinkle with half the crushed walnuts and half the ground coffee.

5. Fold the lower third of the dough onto itself, then fold it over again onto the top third. Repeat steps 4 and 5 with the second piece of dough.

6. Transfer each piece of dough to a baking tray and chill in the freezer for at least 30 minutes; this makes things so much easier to handle at the next step. While the dough is chilling, prepare a Nordic Ware baking sheet (with a lid) by buttering the base and lining it with baking paper. At this point, you can keep one batch of dough in the freezer to bake on another day, if you like, or you can choose to bake both.

7. When you're ready to bake, remove the dough from the freezer and place it on a very lightly floured surface. Use your hands to roll the dough onto itself and form a log, until the dough is sticking together and the seam line is barely visible. With a small, sharp knife, slice the log crossways into 12 even pieces, roughly 3 cm (1¼ inches) thick. You want the spiral of the filling visible in each piece.

8. Tuck the 'tail' underneath each bun, and place them into the lined baking tray with the spiral side up. Allow the buns to proof for at least 1 hour and up to 2 hours at room temperature, covered with the lid or a tea towel.

9. An hour before baking, heat the oven to 200°C (400°F). When the buns are proofed, bake them for 15 minutes, then remove from the oven and sprinkle with the reserved cinnamon sugar mix. Return to the oven and bake for a further 15 minutes until they're a wonderful shade of caramel brown.

10. Remove the buns from the oven, then brush with maple glaze to maximise the sticky, sugary experience. Eat while still warm, with a coffee.

NOTE

You don't want your walnuts to turn to dust, so use a mortar and pestle or stick blender to crush them until they are about pebble-sized.

If you don't have any Nordic Ware proofing trays with lids, simply use baking trays and tea towels to proof and bake.

Challah buns

MAKES 12

These are like a soft milk bun: perfect for kids' lunchboxes, burgers, on the table at a barbecue or to make a killer prawn sandwich. But not, of course, if you're kosher. If that's you, this also happens to be one of the only ways you can have an excellent burger because, unlike milk or brioche buns, there's no dairy.

INGREDIENTS

1 quantity of challah dough (page 114)
1 tablespoon oat milk or water, for glazing
Maple glaze (page 225), for brushing

1. Follow the core challah recipe (page 114) up until the end of step 3, when you're about to divide the dough. At the end of the bulk rise, you should have a dough that is billowy and has doubled in volume.

2. Lightly flour or oil a bench and tip out the dough. Form it into a rough rectangle, caressing it into place with your outstretched hands.

3. With a small, sharp knife or pastry card, score long lines in the rectangle of dough, moving from left to right, leaving approximately 5 cm (2 inches) between each. Now follow the lines to cut the rectangle into strips, then cut the strips into individual pieces that weigh approximately 100 g (3½ oz).

4. Lightly flour your hands. Cup your dominant hand gently over one piece of dough and, while placing some pressure against the dough and bench, rotate your hand clockwise. The bottom of the dough will stick a little, but this is the anchoring point that will help create a bun shape. Continue this until you have a tight, round bun, then transfer to a Nordic Ware proofing tray and repeat with remaining pieces of dough until you've filled up two trays; you should fit six buns nicely in each.

5. Cover the trays, and let the buns stand until they have risen considerably, 45 minutes to 1 hour. If you've only got one tray, either cover the remaining buns with a tea towel, or place them on a baking tray and turn a large plastic container upside down over them.

6. Heat oven to 200°C (400°F). Just before baking, brush your buns with oat milk, completely covering them, then transfer to the oven on trays (remove any lids). Bake the buns for 10 minutes, then rotate each tray and bake for a further 10–13 minutes until golden.

7. Remove the buns from the oven and immediately glaze with maple glaze, then allow to cool. Extra buns can be frozen in snap-lock bags and then thawed the morning you plan to use them.

NOTE

If you don't have any Nordic Ware proofing trays with lids, simply use baking trays and tea towels to proof and bake.

Tin loaf (for your perfect sausage sanga)

MAKES 2 x 600 G (1 LB 5 OZ) LOAVES OR A 1.2 KG (2 LB 12 OZ) LOAF

SPECIAL EQUIPMENT

For 1 large loaf:
Large loaf tin,
  33 x 10 x 10 cm
  (13 x 4 x 4 inches)

For 2 loaves:
Small loaf tins x 2,
  22 x 10 x 10 cm
  (8½ x 4 x 4 inches)

INGREDIENTS

1 quantity of challah
  dough (page 114)
Sunflower oil,
  for greasing
1 tablespoon oat milk or
  water, for glazing
Maple glaze (page 225),
  for brushing

Challah in a tin loaf, you ask? Baking this slightly sweet, enriched dough into a loaf shape gives you something similar to the fluffy Japanese bread shokupan, or those sliced white loaves that were a part of most Western childhoods. Top Melbourne restaurant Attica, down the road from our first bakery, served its possum sausage sizzle on this. We reckon you could do the same with whatever sausage takes your fancy.

1. Follow the core challah recipe (page 114) up until the end of step 3, when you're about to divide the dough. At the end of the bulk rise, you should have a dough that is billowy and has doubled in volume.

2. Lightly flour or oil a bench and tip the dough onto it. Form the dough into a rough rectangle, caressing it into place with your outstretched hands. The short side of the rectangle should face you.

3. If you're using the smaller tin, you need to divide the dough into two equal pieces using your pastry card; weigh them out to ensure they're both 600 g (1 lb 5 oz).

4. Working with one piece of dough at a time (if you're making two loaves), start creating the shape you need for a tin loaf. Visualise your rectangle divided into thirds, running from top to bottom. Fold the top third over itself, and seal this by depressing the dough with your fingers. Then roll this section onto the remaining third of the dough, sealing it and giving you a shape like a log.

5. If your baking tin or tins aren't non-stick, grease them with oil and line them with baking paper. If you're using non-stick, you can place the loaf or loaves in immediately; gently lay them in, remembering the dough will expand to fill the space as it proofs.

6. Cover with a large upturned plastic tub, to prevent a skin forming, and proof at ambient temperature for at least 1 hour. The dough should double in size, if not grow even more.

7. Heat the oven to 200°C (400°F). Glaze the top(s) with oat milk, then, if baking two smaller loaves, bake them for 10 minutes, rotate them, and bake for a further 10 minutes until risen and golden. Alternatively, for the large loaf, bake for 15 minutes then rotate and bake for a further 15 minutes.

8. Remove the loaves from the oven, allow to cool for 10 minutes, then remove from tin(s), place on a wire cooling rack and brush the top(s) with the maple glaze. You're now ready to slice and serve.

Almost Croissants

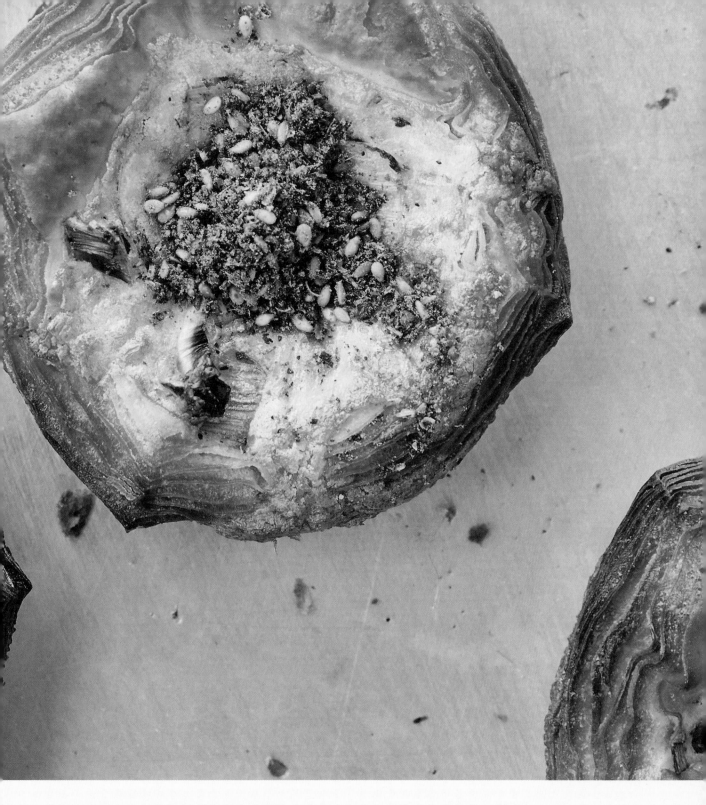

130–153

CROISSANTS AT HOME

Pastries were one of the last things we added to our line-up at Baker Bleu. Customers asked for them all the time, but we simply didn't have room in our first shop; we needed to move to our bigger premises.

A year after being in there, though, because of the success of our pastries we'd run out of room again, so we took on a second lease and moved all of our pastry and viennoiserie production there. People love pastries – what can I say?

Today, our croissants, which are leavened with sourdough starter, are a bestseller. I find, though, that making them at home, with the proofing and humidity required, isn't worth the trouble.

The good news is, you can still make a bunch of amazing pastries using croissant dough. I think that sacrificing the traditional croissant shape is a small price to pay for the intoxicating smell of fresh-baked Danishes, quiches, escargots and other delicious crisp, buttery pastries.

Core croissant dough

MAKES 1.2 KG (2 LB 12 OZ)

I always joke that Baker Bleu is all about not doing things properly. Our vegan challah (page 114) is a great example, while the 'croissants' and Danishes baked in confoil tins (the small aluminium pie tins you put the pastries in) are our way of giving you something like croissants at home. The tins support the pastry, so you don't really need to tackle shaping, and it also means you can fill it with lots of different ingredients, opening up many avenues.

Making laminated pastry dough is still a bit of a process, I'll warn you. There's a lot of resting, chilling and measuring. But if you are the type of person that likes a cooking project, you should find it very rewarding. Be sure to read the tips on page 136 before you begin.

Prepare any fillings for the following pastries while your dough is resting. You'll need to start this recipe 1–2 days ahead.

MAKING THE DOUGH

INGREDIENTS

250 g (9 oz) unsalted butter (for lamination)

Milk poolish
125 ml (4 fl oz) milk
12 g (¼ oz) fresh yeast (or 4 g/⅛ oz dried)
100 g (3½ oz) strong (baker's) flour

Dough
400 g (14 oz) strong (baker's) flour
70 g (2½ oz) raw sugar
10 g (¼ oz) fine pink salt
12 g (¼ oz) fresh yeast (or 4 g/⅛ oz dried)
160 g (5¼ fl oz) milk, at 4°C (39°F)
60 g (2¼ oz) unsalted butter, at room temperature

1. To make the milk poolish, whisk the milk and yeast in a large bowl until dissolved. Add the flour and combine with a spatula, scraping down the sides to ensure everything is mixed well. Cover and leave for an hour at room temperature.

2. After an hour, move the poolish to the fridge and leave it to rest overnight. The next day it should be nicely active, with tiny bubbles on the surface.

3. To prepare the 250 g (9 oz) butter for lamination, remove it from the fridge and leave it at room temperature for 30 minutes. The butter should reach approximately 12°C (55°F) after this time.

4. Cut the butter lengthways into four rectangles of roughly the same thickness, then lay them flat in a single layer with the long edges touching between two sheets of baking paper. Pound the butter with a rolling pin to soften it.

5. Keeping the butter between the baking paper, roll it out to a 20 cm (8 inch) square. To help achieve a perfect square, once the butter flattens, you can fold three sides of the baking paper to create a 20 cm (8 inch) square, then roll the butter into each corner and roll it to an even thickness. Then turn the baking paper 180 degrees and fold the remaining side. With the rolling pin, roll the butter again into each corner of the baking paper. Once complete, store the butter square in the fridge.

6. To make the dough, place the flour, sugar, salt, yeast and cold milk in the bowl of a stand mixer fitted with the dough hook. Add the poolish, then mix for 3 minutes on low speed until combined. Add the softened butter, increase motor to medium speed and mix for 10–12 minutes until the dough is smooth, elastic and strong. Use a probe thermometer to check the temperature of the dough; it should be 22–24°C (72–75°F).

→

If it's warmer than this, transfer the bowl to the fridge for 30 minutes. When the dough is ready, you should be able to see through it when you stretch it with your hands.

7. Shape the dough into a ball and transfer it to a container. Cover with a lid or a tea towel, and leave for 20 minutes at room temperature (23–24°C/73–75°F) to rest.

8. After resting, roll out the dough on a very lightly floured surface to a rectangle measuring 40 x 20 cm (16 x 8 inches) with the long edge facing you (image 01, page 135). Wrap the dough in plastic wrap, place it on a baking tray and chill it in the freezer for 40 minutes. Now, move the tray to the coldest part of the fridge and let it rest for 12 hours (or overnight).

FOLDING AND LAMINATING

1. Remove the butter block from the fridge 20–30 minutes before starting the lamination; the ideal temperature of the butter should be around 12°C (54°F).

2. Remove dough from the fridge, place it on a very lightly floured surface, then unwrap the butter and place it in the centre of the dough (image 02). Fold the top and bottom sides of the dough towards the centre (image 03), then rotate the dough 90 degrees.

3. With a sharp knife, carefully slice through the dough along both of the long sides, using only the very tip of the knife (image 04). You don't want to cut all the way through to the butter. The idea is to release some tension in the dough as you roll.

4. Roll out the dough towards the open ends until the rectangle is 90 cm (35½ inches) in length.

5. Rotate the dough so the long side faces you and visualise the rectangle divided into quarters from left to right. Trim the edges so they're straight, then fold one end (a quarter) of the dough over itself, and the remaining end (three quarters) in, so the two edges meet (image 05). Press the seam where they meet down, then fold one half of the dough onto the other half, so it overlaps, like a book (image 06).

6. With a sharp knife, make a small incision on an angle in each corner, using the tip of your knife (image 07).

7. Cover the dough in plastic wrap and leave it to rest in the freezer for 20 minutes, then move it to the fridge for another 20 minutes.

8. Remove the dough from the fridge, unwrap it and place it back on a lightly floured surface. Roll the dough out towards the open ends until you have a rectangle about 80 cm (31½ inches) in length.

9. Rotate it so the long side faces you, and visualise the dough being made up of thirds, going from left to right (image 08). Now fold a third of the dough into the middle and fold the other third on top, so it overlaps (image 09), then wrap it in plastic wrap.

→

10. If you're planning to use the dough on the same day, rest it in the freezer for 30 minutes followed by 20 minutes in the fridge so it's not too hard or too soft. You can then use it in the recipes in this chapter; don't leave laminated dough in the fridge for more than 2 hours. Alternatively, if you're not ready to use it, you can freeze all or half of the dough (see tips below), but be sure not to leave the dough overnight in the fridge then freeze it later; it's much better to freeze straight after you finish all the folds.

TIPS FOR LAMINATING

- Always roll to the open sides, seam-side up.

- Ensure your room temperature is no higher than 28°C (82°F); it should be as cold as possible.

- Dough temperature for lamination should be around 2°C (36°F).

- To roll the dough evenly, work on the dough in halves; first, roll half the dough out and away from you, then turn the dough 180 degrees, and work on the other half.

TO FREEZE CROISSANT DOUGH

When freezing laminated croissant dough, the following tips should help:

- Dough can be stored in the freezer for up to 10 days.

- Wrap the dough entirely with plastic wrap or in plastic sheets.

- Do not leave the dough overnight in the fridge and freeze it later. It's much better to freeze it straight after you finish all the folds, or to plan to use it all up within 2 hours.

- To use frozen dough, the day before you want to work with it, transfer it from the freezer to the fridge and leave it for at least 12 hours (overnight) to thaw out, covered.

HOW TO CUT A LAMINATED BLOCK OF DOUGH

Some of the recipes to follow will not need the whole quantity of croissant dough. To divide the dough, you'll need to take extra care to avoid damaging the pastry layers you've just created. To halve it:

- Chill the dough after lamination for an hour in the freezer, covered.

- Remove and place the block on a large chopping board, so the open side is facing you.

- Mark the centre of the block using a ruler or rolling pin, then use a large, sharp knife to score a very fine cut from the top towards you in one quick motion, trying to just cut through a single layer. Make sure you don't pull the knife back and forth or you'll damage the layers. Once it's been scored, split the block in half in one smooth motion with the knife.

Christmas croissants
(or lazy mince tarts)

MAKES 16

An example of us taking a shortcut but creating something more than the sum of its parts along the way: a fruit-filled pastry that will have you feeling the Christmas spirit in no time. This was originally created by one of our development chefs, the great JP Twomey, who also worked for many years with Andrew McConnell.

Begin this recipe at least 2 days ahead. You'll need 16 confoil tins.

INGREDIENTS

1.2 kg (2 lb 12 oz) core
   croissant dough
   (page 133), chilled
Oil spray, for greasing
Eggwash (see notes),
   for brushing
Raw sugar, for sprinkling

Fruit mix

100 g (3½ oz) dried
   cherries
100 g (3½ oz) raisins
25 g (1 oz) almond meal
Juice and finely grated
   zest of 1 orange
Juice and finely zest
   of 1 lemon
100 g (3½ oz) dark
   brown sugar
50 g (1¾ oz) mixed peel
4 g (⅛ oz) ground
   cinnamon
4 g (⅛ oz) mixed spice
1 apple, skin on, grated
3 tablespoons
   marmalade
2 tablespoons brandy

1. For the fruit mix, combine all the ingredients in a large bowl and mix well. Squeeze and squish them together with your hands so the fruit has the best opportunity to macerate. Leave this in the fridge, covered, for 2 days, or ideally a week to develop the fullest flavour.

2. On the day you're going to bake, make the almond cream. In a stand mixer fitted with the paddle attachment, cream the butter, sugar and almond meal on medium speed for 3 minutes or until light and creamy; the mix will look white when it's ready. Scrape down the sides of the bowl, then add the egg in two batches, mixing well and scraping down the bowl after each addition. When the egg is fully incorporated, use a spatula to fold in the flour.

3. Lightly dust the surface of your bench with flour and, without applying too much pressure, roll out the croissant dough to a 44 cm (17½ inch) square as evenly as possible. Keep turning the dough as you go to ensure even thickness. Cut the square in half to form two 22 x 44 cm (8½ x 17½ inch) rectangles (or into 4 squares if it won't fit in your fridge), wrap in plastic wrap and chill for 20 minutes.

4. Remove the dough from the fridge and use a small, sharp knife to score a grid of 11 cm (4¼ inch) squares; you should end up with 16 marked squares. Wrap up the dough again and rest it in the freezer for 15 minutes.

5. With a small, sharp knife and a ruler, cut the pastry along the marks. If the dough is getting too soft, place it in the fridge for 20 minutes to firm up.

6. Meanwhile, lightly spray your confoil tins with cooking oil.

7. Once the dough has chilled, pipe 20 g (¾ oz) of almond cream in the centre of each square then top the cream with 35 g (1¼ oz) of fruit mix. Press the filling down gently. It's important to have the filling right in the middle of the square.

Almond cream

140 g (5 oz) unsalted butter, at room temperature

140 g (5 oz) caster (superfine) sugar

140 g (5 oz) almond meal

80 g (2¾ oz) eggs (about 1⅓ eggs), at room temperature

5 g (⅛ oz) plain (all-purpose) or strong (baker's) flour

8. Carefully fold two opposite corners of the pastry over the centre, followed by the other two opposite corners, creating a little parcel that completely covers the filling. You may need to stretch the dough slightly so that the corners overlap in the middle. Press the middle gently so that it seals, then place each parcel into the prepared tins.

9. Create a proofer in your oven by placing a pot with 2 cups (500 ml) of freshly boiled water in the bottom. With the oven off, place a baking tray on the rack directly above the water and place the pastries, in their confoil tins, on the rack above. Close the door and allow the pastries to proof for 2–2.5 hours, or until they double in size. Remove the pastries from the oven and heat it to 185°C (375°F).

10. Brush the pastry parcels with eggwash, sprinkle liberally with raw sugar and bake for 18–20 minutes, until light golden brown. Allow to cool slightly before serving, as the fruit mix will be very hot. Keep extras in a paper bag, and reheat in a 180°C (350°F) oven for 5–10 minutes, brushed with a little water. Or freeze in a snap-lock bag and reheat for a little longer.

NOTES

Save the remaining egg from the almond cream to use as your eggwash at step 10.

If you want to get ahead, you can make the almond cream up to a week before using it. Store it covered in the fridge, and remember to soften it at room temperature for 30 minutes before use.

Automation (or how I learned to stop worrying and love machines)

As much as I love the process of making a loaf of bread by hand and seeing what can come from the care you put into it, I've realised that baking bread commercially is a completely different story.

Lifting hundreds of 25-kilogram flour bags, cleaning out a mixing bowl that holds 200 kilograms of dough, and bending over for 12 or 16 hours at a time, day after day? It's not sustainable to do this manually. I once read that bakers in pre-industrial Europe had a life expectancy of 35 years.

What I get more excited about now is finding a machine that does some of the heavy lifting (literally). It's not about wanting to get rid of people. Baking might be more romanticised now, but you can still count on one hand the kids in a classroom who want to become bakers.

It's a fact that if you want to make a lot of bread, and make it well, this is how it's got to be.

There'll be bakers out there who will say that I've lost the passion for it, or Baker Bleu is not artisan anymore. Go to Europe and plenty of great bakeries use machines. It's normal. It's not anything to be frowned upon.

It was at Iggy's Down Under that I first saw the possibilities of using machines to make artisan bread in large volumes. My obsessive nature kicked in: I wanted to learn everything I could about the processes.

As soon as I could get a forklift at Baker Bleu to lift our pallets of flour, I got one. That was two years in. Six months in, I got a hydraulic divider to portion huge batches of dough into precise loaves. A few months later we had a moulder.

It was crazy how much equipment we squeezed into this tiny bakery. But it made our production so much faster.

In 2020, when Australia's borders were closed, I realised we were about to have a massive staff shortage. We ordered an enormous manufacturing line for our bigger bakery that weighs, moulds, proofs and bakes the bread for us. We don't shape anything by hand. We don't load the oven manually. Even during huge spikes of COVID cases, we were able to bake bread every day because of this manufacturing line.

Today, with such severe staff shortages in hospitality, you have to market yourself as an employer. At our bakery, people know there'll be less lifting. They know they're not going to be ruining their body the way they might at a bakery that hand-weighs, hand-shapes and so on.

The funny thing is, I'm not technical at all. Some bakers can tell you about the pH content of their starter and the scientific side of bread-making. That's not me.

But I do believe that technology is how you can grow in baking today.

There's no way I would have opened a bakery in a city I don't live in without this stuff. I still have so much control over the bread even when I'm not there.

Through an app on my phone, I can see the temperature of the proofers and the ovens.

Through an app on my phone, I can see the temperature of the proofers and the ovens. I can tweak things if I think something is proofing too quickly or slowly. We're all on Microsoft Teams, so at the end of the day, the people on that shift can send an update with photos of the product and I can see how it looks.

You can't solely rely on the technology to give you a great product. But it makes life a hell of a lot easier for you and your staff.

Baklava escargots

MAKES 17

Melbourne's food scene is vibrant, with many different cultures continuing their own traditions from back home and sharing them with new audiences. It makes eating (and cooking) in this city exciting, with loads of inspiration wherever you look.

This little pastry captures all of that. It takes the classic French pastry shape of a pain aux raisins (or escargot), the Middle Eastern dessert of baklava and the Persian sweet treat, halva, and twists them into a fruit-free, nut-studded pastry.

INGREDIENTS

1.1 kg (2 lb 7 oz) core croissant dough (page 133), chilled
250 g (9 oz) pastry cream (page 225)
Shredded halva, to garnish (see note)

White chocolate and halva crumble

150 g (5½ oz) walnuts
150 g (5½ oz) white chocolate, roughly chopped
125 g (4½ oz) pistachio halva

Orange blossom syrup

130 g (4¾ oz) raw sugar
100 g (3½ oz) water
½ teaspoon orange blossom water

1. For the white chocolate and halva crumble, combine the walnuts and white chocolate in a food processor and use the pulse function until you have a coarsely ground mix. Roughly chop the pistachio halva with a knife, then add it to the walnut-white chocolate mix and stir to combine.

2. For the orange blossom syrup, combine the sugar and water in a saucepan over high heat and stir occasionally until it comes to the boil. Take off the heat, cool briefly, then stir in the orange blossom water.

3. Roll out your chilled croissant dough on a lightly floured bench to a 44 x 36 cm (17½ x 14¼ inch) rectangle, with the short side facing you.

4. With a palette knife, spread an even layer of pastry cream on the dough, spreading it all the way to the edges, except for the top edge, where you'll leave a 2 cm (¾ inch) border.

5. Sprinkle the white chocolate and halva crumble evenly over the dough.

6. Starting from the side closest to you, use your hands to roll the dough into a log, rolling it gently but tightly towards the border at the top. Try to keep the pressure as even as possible. Once you reach the border, stop rolling, leaving a 'tail' with no cream. Transfer the log to a baking tray, cover with paper towel and place it in the fridge for 30 minutes to firm up.

7. Remove the dough from the fridge and use a serrated knife to cut it crossways into 2 cm (¾ inch) slices, each weighing 100 g (3½ oz). You want each slice to have a spiral pattern as the cross section.

8. Gently stretch the tails (the part without any cream) and tuck them under, pressing them onto the base of each piece. Place the escargots on a baking tray lined with baking paper, allowing enough space for them to spread while baking.

9. Create a proofer in your oven by placing a pot with 2 cups (500 ml) of freshly boiled water in the bottom. With the oven off, place a baking tray on the rack above the water, then place the tray with the pastries on the rack above. Close the door and allow the pastries to proof for 2.5–3 hours or until they double in size. Remove pastries from the oven and heat it to 185°C (375°F).

10. Bake escargots for 22–25 minutes or until light golden. Remove, then brush them with orange blossom syrup and sprinkle with shredded halva. Reheat extras in a 180°C (350°F) oven for 5–10 minutes, brushed with a little water.

NOTE

Shredded halva is available from Middle Eastern grocers or specialty food stores. If you can't find it, use extra pistachio halva that you've chopped or crumbled.

Apple and ricotta Danishes

MAKES 16

The Danish gets a bad rap, thanks to the soft, flabby, oversized ones with a too-sweet glaze that sub-standard bakeries sell. This version, with loads of flaky pastry layers, should erase any doubts. You'll need 16 confoil tins.

INGREDIENTS

1.2 kg (2 lb 12 oz) core croissant dough (page 133), chilled

Apple filling
40 g (1½ oz) butter
50 g (1¾ oz) caster (superfine) sugar
600 g (1 lb 5 oz) Granny Smith apples (about 3 apples), peeled, quartered and cut into 2 cm (¾ inch) dice
⅛ teaspoon ground cinnamon

Ricotta cream
170 g (6 oz) pastry cream (page 225)
240 g (9 oz) ricotta
20 g (¾ oz) caster (superfine) sugar

Pecan crumble
100 g (3½ oz) pecans
70 g (2½ oz) butter, at room temperature
45 g (1¾ oz) soft brown sugar
45 g (1¾ oz) caster (superfine) sugar
90 g (3¼ oz) plain (all-purpose) flour
¼ teaspoon ground cinnamon

1. For the apple filling, melt the butter and sugar in a saucepan on low heat and cook, swirling occasionally, until a light golden caramel forms, about 6–8 minutes. Add the apple, mix well, then increase the heat to medium and cook, giving it a gentle stir or swirl now and then, until soft and golden, about 12 minutes. Stir in the cinnamon and remove from the heat. Drain off excess liquid through a sieve, then cool completely before use.

2. For the ricotta cream, place the pastry cream, ricotta and sugar in a large bowl and whisk until combined. Keep in the fridge until ready to use.

3. For the pecan crumble, place the pecans in a food processor and pulse until they resemble coarse breadcrumbs. Add the butter to a stand mixer fitted with the paddle attachment and beat on medium speed for about 3 minutes until creamy. Add both the sugars and mix for 2 minutes, then add the flour and cinnamon and mix slowly until coarse crumbs form. Stop mixing and use your fingers to break the crumble into uniform, pebble-sized pieces. Toss the pecans through the crumble and set aside.

4. Roll out your chilled croissant dough as evenly as possible on a lightly floured bench to a 45 cm (18 inch) square; try not to apply too much pressure and keep turning the dough to ensure even thickness. Cut the square in half (into two equal rectangles), wrap in plastic wrap and chill for 20 minutes to rest.

5. Remove the dough from the fridge and with a sharp knife, score a grid of 11 cm (4¼ inch) squares; you should end up with 16 marked squares. Rest the scored dough in the freezer for 15 minutes.

6. With a small, sharp knife and a ruler, cut the pastry along the marks. If the dough is getting too soft, place it in the fridge for 20 minutes to firm up.

7. Line your confoil tins by placing each square over the centre and gently pressing the pastry into it. Ensure you push the dough right into the edges. Fill each shell with 25 g (1 oz) of ricotta cream and place each tin on a baking tray.

8. Create a proofer in your oven by placing a pot with 2 cups (500 ml) of freshly boiled water in the bottom. With the oven off, place a baking tray on the rack above the water and place the pastries, in their confoil tins, on the rack above. Close the door and allow pastries to proof for 2–2.5 hours or until they double in size. Remove pastries from the oven and heat to it 185°C (375°F).

9. Place a scoop (20 g/¾ oz or so) of apples on top of the ricotta cream, followed by a generous scoop (about 15 g/½ oz) of pecan crumble.

10. Bake for 20 minutes or until the pastry is golden brown. Cool, then pop the pastries out of the tins to serve. Keep extras in a paper bag, and reheat in a 180°C (350°F) oven for 5–10 minutes, brushed with a little water. Or freeze in a snap-lock bag and reheat for a little longer.

Blueberry cheesecake Danishes

MAKES 16

We've upped the indulgence factor on this pastry, combining two desserts in one. The crunch of the pastry replaces the biscuit base on a cheesecake, and the tart blueberries echo the tang of the sour cream. Serve this at the end of a meal, or as the sweet highlight of a big brunch spread. You'll need 16 confoil tins.

INGREDIENTS

1.1 kg (2 lb 7 oz) core croissant dough (page 133), chilled
250 g (9 oz) fresh blueberries

Cheesecake filling

250 g (9 oz) cream cheese, at room temperature
140 g (5 oz) raw sugar
Finely grated zest of 1 lemon
75 g (2¾ oz) eggs (about 1.5 eggs)
15 g (½ oz) strong (baker's) flour
125 g (4½ oz) thick (double) cream
125 g (4½ oz) sour cream

1. Heat the oven to 120°C (235°F).

2. Meanwhile, place the cream cheese, sugar and lemon zest in the bowl of a stand mixer fitted with the paddle attachment and beat for 4 minutes on medium speed until light and fluffy.

3. Add the egg slowly, beating well after each addition and scraping down the sides regularly. Once the egg is fully incorporated, add the flour and beat until smooth. Add the cream and sour cream and beat for 2 minutes on medium speed until incorporated.

4. Line a 23 cm (9 inch) square baking tray with a lip with baking paper. Pour the cheesecake mixture into the tray and bake for 40 minutes. Test if it's ready by shaking the tray; it should be set. Cool briefly, then place in the fridge to chill for at least 3 hours or overnight.

5. Once it's thoroughly chilled, break the cheesecake up into pieces and blend it in a food processor, scraping down the sides regularly, until completely smooth. Transfer to a bowl, cover the surface with plastic wrap and refrigerate until ready to use (up to 5 days).

6. Roll out your chilled croissant dough as evenly as possible on a lightly floured bench to a 45 cm (18 inch) square; try not to apply too much pressure and keep turning the dough to ensure even thickness. Cut the square in half (into two rectangles), wrap in plastic wrap and chill for 20 minutes to rest.

7. Remove the dough from the fridge and, with a sharp knife, score a grid of 11 cm (4¼ inch) squares; you should end up with 16 marked squares. Wrap up the scored dough, and rest it in the freezer for 15 minutes.

8. With a small, sharp knife and a ruler, cut the pastry along the marks. If the dough is getting too soft, place it in the fridge for 20 minutes to firm up.

9. Line your confoil tins by placing each square over the centre and gently pressing the pastry into it. Ensure you push the dough right into the edges. Fill each tin with 30 g (1 oz) of cheesecake filling and place each lined tin on a baking tray.

10. Create a proofer in your oven by placing a pot with 2 cups (500 ml) of freshly boiled water in the bottom. With the oven off, place a baking tray on the rack above the water and place the pastries, in their confoil tins, on the rack above. Close the door and allow the pastries to proof for 2–2.5 hours or until doubled in size. Remove the pastries from the oven and heat to it 185°C (375°F).

11. Bake the pastries for 18–20 minutes until golden and the filling is set. Allow to cool for 15–20 minutes, then top with fresh blueberries.

Leek and za'atar confoil quiches

MAKES 16

A spring picnic would be the perfect occasion for these savoury, leek-filled pastries. Just the right size for one person, or easily cut in half to stretch further, they're bound to impress. You'll need 16 confoil tins.

INGREDIENTS

1.2 kg (2 lb 12 oz) core croissant dough (page 133), chilled
80 g (2¾ oz) za'atar, plus extra for sprinkling
480 g (1 lb 1 oz) three-cheese mix (page 224)

Quiche filling
150 g (5½ oz) eggs (about 3 eggs)
60 g (2¼ oz) egg yolk (from about 3½ eggs)
360 g (12¾ oz) thick (double) cream
½ teaspoon salt

Marinated leeks
2 leeks, trimmed, halved and cut into 1 cm (½ inch) slices
1 tablespoon za'atar
¼ cup (60 ml) olive oil

1. For the marinated leeks, mix the leek with the za'atar and olive oil, season with a grind of two of black pepper, and leave to marinate for 1 hour.

2. To make the quiche filling, combine the eggs, egg yolk, cream and salt in a bowl or jug and blend with a stick blender (or whisk) until well combined, then pass through a sieve. Chill until needed.

3. Roll out your chilled croissant dough as evenly as possible on a lightly floured bench to a 45 cm (18 inch) square; try not to apply too much pressure and keep turning the dough to ensure even thickness. Cut the square in half (into two equal rectangles), wrap in plastic wrap and chill for 20 minutes to rest.

4. Remove the dough from the fridge and, with a sharp knife, score a grid of 11 cm (4¼ inch) squares; you should end up with 16 marked squares. Wrap up the scored dough, and rest it in the freezer for 15 minutes.

5. With a small, sharp knife and a ruler, cut the pastry along the marks. If the dough is getting too soft, place it in the fridge for 20 minutes to firm up.

6. Line your confoil tins by placing each square over the centre of the tin and gently pressing the pastry into it. Ensure you push the dough right into the edges of the base. Place lined tins on a baking tray.

7. Create a proofer in your oven by placing a pot with 2 cups (500 ml) of freshly boiled water in the bottom. With the oven off, place a baking tray on the rack above the water and place the pastries, in their confoil tins, on the rack above. Close the door and allow the pastries to proof for 2–2.5 hours or until doubled in size. Remove the pastries from the oven and heat to it 185°C (375°F).

8. Press the pastry right into the edge of the tins again, then fill each pastry with 30 g (1 oz) of marinated leek, 1 teaspoon of za'atar and 25 g (1 oz) of cheese mix. Pour the chilled quiche filling slowly into the pastries, and top with another tablespoon of cheese mix.

9. Bake the quiches for 22–27 minutes until the pastry is golden and the filling is set. Sprinkle some extra za'atar on top before serving.

Mushroom, béchamel and ricotta salata Danishes

MAKES 16

This is on the richer end of the pastries we offer, but the combination of tender, buttery mushrooms with a cheesy sauce is one for the ages. I dare you to resist one of these on a cool autumn morning. You'll need 16 confoil tins.

INGREDIENTS

1.1 kg (2 lb 7 oz) core croissant dough (page 133), chilled
160 g (5¾ oz) ricotta salata, shaved into strips with a peeler
12 chives, thinly sliced

Mushroom base

500 g (1 lb 2 oz) mixed mushrooms (we suggest an equal mix of Swiss brown, button and oyster mushrooms), thinly sliced
⅓ cup (80 ml) olive oil
30 g (1 oz) unsalted butter, melted
2 garlic cloves, roughly chopped
1 thyme sprig
1 cinnamon stick
Finely grated zest of 1 lemon

Béchamel

40 g (1½ oz) butter
30 g (1 oz) strong (baker's) flour
300 g (10½ oz) milk, warmed to 50°C (120°F)
¼ teaspoon freshly grated nutmeg
40 g (1½ oz) three-cheese mix (page 224)

1. For the mushroom base, add all the ingredients to a large bowl, mix well, then season to taste with salt and pepper and mix again.

2. Heat the oven to 200°C (400°F). Spread the mushroom mix in a single layer on a non-stick baking tray (you may need to use several baking trays or bake this in batches) and bake for 10–13 minutes or until the mushrooms are tender. Discard thyme and cinnamon. Cool completely before use.

3. For the béchamel, melt the butter in a saucepan over medium heat, add the flour and whisk for 1 minute. Still whisking, gradually pour in the warm milk. Once all the milk is added, bring to the boil and cook, whisking frequently to prevent the base catching, until the béchamel is thick, but still holds a runny consistency. Add the nutmeg and the cheese mix, and stir well with a wooden spoon until combined. Transfer the sauce to a bowl, cover the surface directly with plastic wrap and refrigerate until ready to use.

4. Roll out your chilled croissant dough as evenly as possible on a lightly floured bench to a 45 cm (18 inch) square; try not to apply too much pressure and keep turning the dough to ensure even thickness. Cut the square in half (into two equal rectangles), wrap in plastic wrap and chill for 20 minutes to rest.

5. Remove the dough from the fridge and with a sharp knife, score a grid of 11 cm (4¼ inch) squares; you should end up with 16 marked squares. Wrap up the scored dough, and rest it in the freezer for 15 minutes.

6. With a small, sharp knife and a ruler, cut the pastry along the marks. If the dough is getting too soft, place it in the fridge for 20 minutes to firm up.

7. Line your confoil tins by placing each square over the centre of the tin and gently pressing the pastry into it. Ensure you push the dough right into the edges of the base. Place the lined tins on a baking tray.

8. Fill each tin with 15 g (½ oz) of béchamel, followed by a large spoonful (about 25 g/1 oz) of the mushroom mix, and another 10 g (¼ oz) of béchamel. (Alternatively, mix approximately 400 g/14 oz of béchamel with 400 g/14 oz of mushroom mix and fill each tin with the mix.)

9. Create a proofer in your oven by placing a pot with 2 cups (500 ml) of freshly boiled water in the bottom. With the oven off, place a baking tray on the rack above the water and place the pastries, in their confoil tins, on the rack above. Close the door and allow the pastries to proof for 2–2.5 hours or until doubled in size. Remove the pastries from the oven and heat to it 185°C (375°F).

10. Bake the pastries for 18–20 minutes until light golden. Remove from oven and allow to cool for 10–15 minutes, then sprinkle with ricotta salata and chives.

Vegemite twists

MAKES 12 TWISTS

Most Australian kids will remember getting Vegemite and cheese scrolls after school from one of the large bakery chains that dot nearly every suburb. It's a bit of a nostalgic treat.

We honour the unbeatable combination of sweet, salty and umami here, although with what I'd dare to say is much better quality cheese, and in a rectangular shape instead of a spiral. We hope it takes you back to your youth.

INGREDIENTS

1.1 kg (2 lb 7 oz) core croissant dough (page 133), chilled
450 g (1 lb) three-cheese mix (page 224)

Vegemite glaze

100 g (3½ oz) Vegemite
25 g (1 oz) boiling water

1. For the Vegemite glaze, weigh the Vegemite directly into a heatproof vessel, such as a glass bowl or measuring jug. Pour the boiling water over it and blitz it all with a stick blender for 2 minutes, or until glossy and slightly runny. Store in the fridge until ready to use.

2. Roll out the croissant dough on a lightly floured bench to a 30 x 48 cm (12 x 19 inch) rectangle.

3. With the short edge facing you, cut the rectangle in half from top to bottom with a sharp knife. Brush one piece with water and place the other piece on top, like a sandwich. The dough should now be 15 cm (6 inches) wide and 48 cm (19 inches) long.

4. Now cut the dough horizontally into 4 cm strips, leaving you with 12 strips of 4 x 15 cm (1½ x 6 inches)

5. Next, cut lengthways through the middle part of each strip, leaving a 1 cm (½ inch) border uncut at each end (that is, your cut should measure 13 cm/5 inches).

6. Take hold of each end of the dough and twist one end of the strip twice in the same direction followed by the other end once in the opposite direction. Hold for approximately a minute so the twist doesn't unravel, then place each twist onto a baking tray lined with baking paper.

7. Create a proofer in your oven by placing a pot with 2 cups (500 ml) of freshly boiled water in the bottom. With the oven off, place a baking tray on the rack above the water and place the pastries on the rack above. Close the door and allow the pastries to proof for 2–3 hours, or until doubled in size. Remove the twists from the oven and heat to it 185°C (375°F).

8. Place 35–40 g (1¼–1½ oz) of three-cheese mix in the centre of each twist, then place the filled twists in the oven and bake for 20–22 minutes until light golden brown.

9. Remove the twists from the oven and, while they're still warm, brush the twists liberally with the Vegemite glaze; the glaze will set as the pastries cool. Wait approximately 20 minutes before serving.

MINI PROJECT

Brioche

MAKES ABOUT 12 BUNS OR 2 LOAVES (ABOUT 600 G/1 LB 5 OZ EACH)

This recipe will make a Parker House-style roll. You know: the soft, buttery bread rolls that arrive golden and warm from the oven, so satisfying to tear apart. They're also a great burger bun.

If you're after a faster result, you can make a brioche tin loaf (see the variation on page 157), which is perfect for a sausage sanga with onions and all the trimmings at home.

When making brioche, it's essential that all the ingredients are at the correct temperature. Take the butter out 2 hours before mixing, but ensure your milk and eggs are used straight from the fridge so they're chilled.

When you're baking, keep an eye on the base so you don't burn the bottom of the rolls. You want each roll to be soft and unctuous.

BAKING INGREDIENTS AND PERCENTAGES		
Strong (baker's) flour	600 g (1 lb 5 oz)	100%
Caster (superfine) sugar	85 g (3 oz)	14%
Fine pink salt	13 g (½ oz)	2.2%
Dried yeast (or 27 g/1 oz fresh)	9 g (¼ oz)	1.5%
Eggs (about 3½)	180 g (6½ oz)	30%
Milk	230 g (8½ oz)	38%
Unsalted butter, at room temperature (about 18°C/64°F)	130 g (4¾ oz)	21.7%

EXTRA INGREDIENTS

Oil spray, for greasing
Sesame seeds (optional), to garnish

Eggwash
50 g (1¾ oz) egg (about 1 egg)
50 g (1¾ oz) egg yolk (from about 2½ eggs)
1 tablespoon milk
¼ teaspoon salt

1. Place the flour, sugar, salt and yeast in a stand mixer fitted with the dough hook attachment and mix for approximately 1 minute (image 01).

2. In a separate bowl, break up the eggs with a whisk, then whisk in the milk before adding this to the flour mix. Use a spatula to combine the two, ensuring there's no flour left at the bottom of the bowl.

3. Mix in the stand mixer on medium speed for 3 minutes or until the dough comes together (image 02).

→

4. Divide the butter into three equal pieces, then with the motor still running, break up one piece and add it to the mix, letting the machine knead it in, ensuring the butter is incorporated well after each addition and scraping down the sides of the bowl (image 03). After the final addition, mix for a further 4 minutes until incorporated.

5. Test if the dough is ready by taking a small piece and stretching it (image 04). If you can see through it, the dough is glossy and all the butter is well incorporated, with no chunks, it's ready to be rested.

6. Transfer the dough to a large bowl lightly sprayed with oil. Cover with plastic wrap and refrigerate overnight to bulk ferment.

7. The next day, tip the dough onto a lightly floured surface and de-gas the dough by making a fist with your hand and pushing it gently yet firmly into the centre of the dough, deflating it.

8. Lightly flour your kitchen scale. Use your pastry card to portion the dough into 100 g (3½ oz) pieces, then leave them to rest on the bench, covered with a tea towel or plastic wrap, for 10 minutes.

9. Shape each piece of dough into a ball by using the dumpling method (page 48) to fold all edges of the dough into the centre until the ball is sealed. Flip them over so the seam side is down. Place your palm over the top of a ball and gently roll it against the bench into a smooth, even ball. Try not to use flour at this stage. Repeat to make 12 balls. At this stage you can continue with this method, or make a tin loaf with the variation opposite.

10. Place the dough balls, just touching each other, on a baking tray lined with baking paper.

11. Create a proofer in your oven by placing a pot with 2 cups (500 ml) of freshly boiled water in the bottom. With the oven off, place a baking tray on the rack above the water, then place the tray of brioche rolls on the rack above it. Close the door and allow the rolls to proof for 1.5–2 hours or until approximately doubled in size. Remove the rolls from the oven and heat it to 180°C (350°F).

12. Whisk all eggwash ingredients together and strain through a fine sieve. Store in the fridge, covered, until you're ready to bake (see note).

13. Before baking, gently brush the buns with an even layer of eggwash, scatter with sesame seeds (if using) then bake for approximately 15 minutes, until dark golden brown. Extra buns can be frozen in snap-lock bags and thawed the morning you plan to use them.

TIN LOAF VARIATION

SPECIAL EQUIPMENT

2 rectangular loaf tins,
22.5 x 14 x 9 cm
(9 x 5½ x 3½ inch)

1. To make a tin loaf, follow the brioche recipe up to the end of step 9 to make your balls of dough (you should have 12), then spray or brush a thin layer of cooking oil on the inside and edges of your loaf tins.

2. Place six balls closely together in one of the tins. You should get two rows of three balls. Repeat for the second tin.

3. Create a proofer in your oven by placing a pot with 2 cups (500 ml) of freshly boiled water in the bottom. With the oven off, place a baking tray on the rack above the water, then place the tins on the rack above it. Close the door and allow the brioche to proof for 2.5–3 hours or until approximately doubled in size. Remove the tins from the oven and heat it to 180°C (350°F).

4. Whisk the eggwash ingredients together and strain through a fine sieve. Store in the fridge, covered, until you're ready to bake (see note).

5. Before baking, gently brush each loaf with an even layer of eggwash, then bake for 15–18 minutes until dark golden brown.

NOTE

Eggwash will keep for
3 days in the fridge.

Orange-chocolate brioche buns

MAKES 16

Brioche is by definition much sweeter than other breads, especially the kind of sourdough loaves that we sell at our bakeries. But that sweetness makes brioche versatile. It can easily be adapted for desserts, as you'll see here with this sweet spin on brioche buns.

The orange purée creates an extra-soft texture inside, and means the citrus flavour permeates every bite. If you love the combination of chocolate and orange, you'll find these are a winner.

INGREDIENTS

1 orange, washed
1 quantity of brioche
  dough ingredients
  (page 155)
130 g (4¾ oz) dark
  chocolate, roughly
  chopped

Eggwash

50 g (1¾ oz) egg
  (about 1 egg)
50 g (1¾ oz) egg yolk
  (from about 2½ eggs)
1 tablespoon milk
¼ teaspoon salt

1. Chop the orange roughly, skin and all, and place it in the bowl of a food processor. Blend until you have a fairly smooth paste.

2. Follow steps 1 and 2 of the brioche recipe (page 155), but add 110 g (3¾ oz) of orange purée to the eggs along with the milk and whisk to combine. Continue with the rest of step 2, then follow steps 3 to 5.

3. If your dough looks ready, add the chopped chocolate and mix on slow speed for 2 minutes until it's incorporated.

4. Transfer the dough to a large bowl lightly sprayed with oil. Cover with plastic wrap and refrigerate overnight to bulk ferment.

5. Tip the dough onto a lightly floured work surface and de-gas the dough by making a fist with your hand and pushing it gently yet firmly into the centre of the dough, deflating it.

6. Lightly flour your kitchen scale and bench. Use your pastry card to portion the dough into 90 g (3¼ oz) pieces and leave to rest on the bench, covered, for 10 minutes. Shape each piece of dough into a ball by using the dumpling method (page 48) to fold all edges of the dough into the centre until the ball is sealed. Flip them over so the seam side is down. Place your palm over the top of a ball and gently roll it against the bench into a smooth, even ball. Try not to use flour at this stage. Repeat with the remaining dough pieces.

7. Place the dough balls, just touching each other, on a baking tray lined with baking paper.

8. Create a proofer in your oven by placing a pot with 2 cups (500 ml) of freshly boiled water in the bottom. With the oven off, place a baking tray on the rack above the water, then place the tray of brioche rolls on the rack above it. Close the door and allow the rolls to proof for 1.5–2 hours or until approximately doubled in size. Remove the rolls from the oven and heat it to 180°C (350°F).

9. Whisk the eggwash ingredients together and strain through a fine sieve. Store in the fridge, covered, until you're ready to bake (see note).

10. Before baking, gently brush the buns with an even layer of eggwash, then bake for 12–15 minutes, until dark golden brown.

NOTE

Eggwash will keep for 3 days in the fridge.

Pies & Cookies

160–175

Sweet khorasan pie dough

MAKES 2 x 18 CM (7 INCH) PIES

SPECIAL EQUIPMENT

2 x aluminium or
cast-iron pie tins,
18 cm (7 inches)
in diameter

One of the golden rules of making shortcrust pastry such as this is to avoid overdeveloping the dough, otherwise you won't get the flakiness that makes it so desirable. Apple-cider vinegar is your secret weapon in achieving that texture. It has a counteractive effect on gluten development so will prevent any toughness from creeping in. More importantly, it also adds a lovely tart edge to sweet items. With the nutty flavour of the khorasan, you'll find this recipe tastes a little different to your average shortcrust; although we use it for pies, it's also a great base for sable biscuits and tarts, including chocolate or caramel.

A couple of things to keep in mind: it's really crucial that you have large, almost coin-sized, shards of butter through the dough. Then when you're mixing the dough, bring it just beyond still being raggedy and falling apart – overmixing destroys the flakiness you get from the big pieces of butter.

BAKING INGREDIENTS AND PERCENTAGES		
Unsalted butter, plus extra for greasing	460 g (1 lb 1 oz)	60%
Filtered water	200 g (7 oz)	26%
Khorasan flour (see note)	770 g (1 lb 11 oz)	100%
Fine pink salt	8 g (¼ oz)	1%
Apple-cider vinegar	20 g (¾ oz)	2.6%
Raw sugar, plus extra for sprinkling	115 g (4 oz)	15%

EXTRA INGREDIENTS

Filling (see options on pages 166 and 168)

1. Your first priority is to chill all the ingredients that need to be cold. Dice the butter into roughly 2 cm (¾ inch) cubes, then place it in the fridge for 40 minutes to 1 hour (if you're short on time, you can get away with half that time). Measure the water into a large jug and also place it in the fridge.

2. Add the flour and salt to a large mixing bowl and whisk to combine. Add the chilled butter and begin to combine things by squeezing the butter and dry ingredients together with your fingertips (image 01). The flour will start to coat the butter and, after a couple of minutes, the whole mix will start to look shaggy (image 02). It's important not to overmix the dough, so keep an eye on things; when it's ready, you should be able to see discs of butter coated in flour.

3. Remove the chilled water from the fridge. Add the vinegar and sugar to the water and whisk them all together thoroughly so the sugar dissolves.

NOTE

If you can't find khorasan flour, baker's flour will also give a fine result.

→

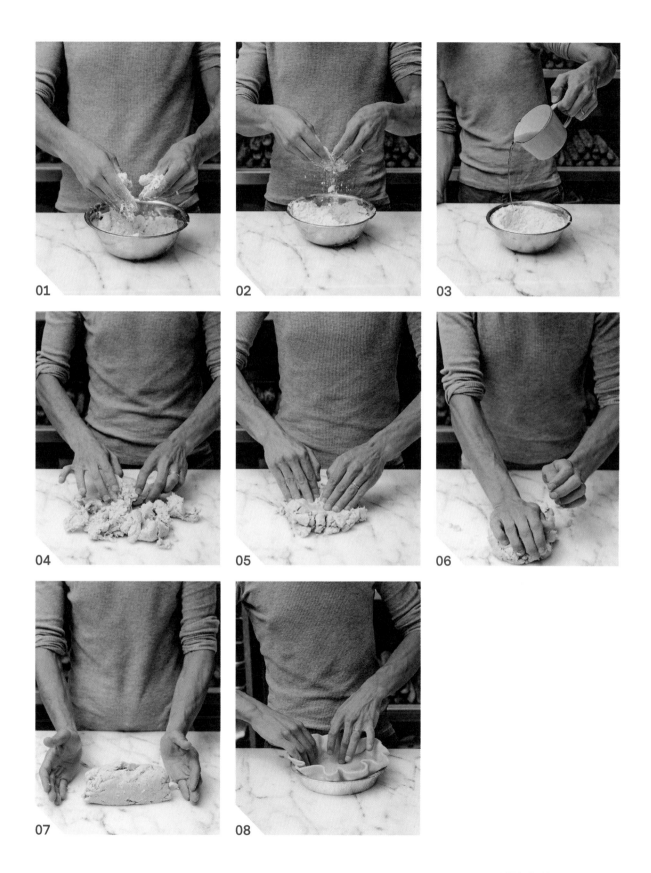

4. Create a well in the centre of your shaggy flour-butter mix, and pour in half the vinegar mixture (image 03). Start to incorporate the shaggy dough with your hand, working first in the centre, then slowly working outwards towards the edge of the bowl. As a dough begins to form, gradually add the rest of the liquid. You may not need it all; this is a dough that should look on the dry side, but once you bake it, the coarse bits of butter will release moisture, so it's better to add less liquid now. It should still look scraggly.

5. Once the pastry has just come together (again, avoid overmixing), you should be able to see the shards of butter in it. This will be your flakiness. Form the dough into a loose rectangle (images 04–07), cover well with plastic wrap or a bag and refrigerate for 1 hour to rest.

6. Remove the dough from the fridge, dust your bench with flour and, with the longest side facing you, start rolling out the dough with a floured rolling pin or wine bottle. Continue rolling until you start to see the edge of the dough form cracks. As soon as this happens, rotate the dough 90 degrees.

7. Continue with this rolling and rotating method until you've rolled the dough to 3 mm ($\frac{1}{8}$ inch) thick. As you're rolling, make sure that the dough isn't sticking to the bench and that it's not getting sticky or warm on your rolling pin. If it is, transfer it to the freezer on a tray for a few minutes (no more than 5 minutes), to firm back up.

8. Once the dough is rolled out, take your pie tin and place it upside down on top of the dough to use as a cutting guide. Cut around the pie tin with a sharp knife, ensuring you've added 2.5 cm (1 inch) of buffer around the circumference to allow for shrinkage. You should easily get two pie cases out of this recipe, or you can make a lid or a lattice.

   To make a lid, roll approximately 200 g (7 oz) of pastry to 2 mm ($\frac{1}{16}$ inch) thickness, in a circular shape. Place an empty pie tin on your pastry (right-way up) and cut around it like a template, then take this piece of dough, put it on a tray and place it in the fridge to chill for 20 minutes.

   To cut strips for a lattice, gather up the dough scraps and form them into a ball, then chill for 5 minutes in the freezer (if you're baking the same day; otherwise freeze it and thaw before use). Roll out the scraps into a rectangle, 3 mm ($\frac{1}{8}$ inch) thick. With a sharp knife, cut strips about 2.5 cm (1 inch) wide and set aside, covered with a tea towel.

   Set the pie shell(s) and/or the lid aside (if you've made two shells and don't want to bake two pies now, freeze one shell).

9. Heat the oven to 170°C (325°F). Grease the inside of your pie tin (I like to use the packaging that's left over from the diced butter). Line the tin with one of the pastry shells (image 08), pushing it into the edges gently with your thumbs, then gently up against the walls of the tin. At this point you can leave the pie shell in the fridge overnight (covered) if you like and you can roll out and cut the lattice the next day.

10. Fill the pie with your chosen filling, top it with a lid or a lattice, and bake as per the recipes on page 166 and 168.

Salted caramel apple pie

MAKES 2 x 18 CM (7 INCH) PIES

Apple and caramel are great friends. Throw them into a pie that uses our nutty khorasan shortcrust pastry for the base, and you've got a toasty winter dessert. A dollop of good cream is pretty much non-negotiable.

INGREDIENTS

1 quantity of khorasan pie dough, formed into a shell, with lid or strips (page 162)
1 egg, lightly beaten
Raw sugar, for sprinkling

Apple filling

1.4 kg (3 lb 2 oz) Granny Smith apples (about 10–12), unpeeled and washed
145 g (5 oz) raw sugar
20 g (¾ oz) strong (baker's) or plain (all-purpose) flour
8 g (¼ oz) ground cinnamon
6 g (⅛ oz) ground allspice
3 g (¹⁄₁₆ oz) freshly grated nutmeg
2 drops Angostura bitters
1 tablespoon lemon juice

Salted caramel

255 g (9¼ oz) caster (superfine) sugar
65 g (2¼ oz) water
130 g (4¾ oz) unsalted butter, diced, at room temperature
130 g (4¾ oz) pure (single) cream
12 g (½ oz) sea salt flakes

NOTE

If you have leftover filling, use it to make stewed apples for porridge, or turn it into mini pies using any scraps of pie dough.

1. To prepare the apple filling, halve and core the apples, then cut them into 5 mm (¼ inch) slices. This is best done with a mandoline, but a very sharp knife is fine if you don't have one. Place the slices in a large bowl with the remaining apple filling ingredients, mix well, and leave at room temperature to macerate for approximately 2 hours.

2. For the salted caramel, put the sugar in a large heavy-based saucepan and pour in the water. Give it a quick stir, then place the saucepan over medium-high heat and cook, stirring, until the sugar has dissolved. (If the sugar is sticking to the sides of the pan, you can use a pastry brush dipped in water to brush down the sides.) Carefully add the butter, swirl the pan a couple of times, and continue cooking, without stirring, until the mixture turns golden brown. Remove from the heat.

3. Meanwhile, warm the cream either by heating it in the microwave (heat it for 50 seconds, stir, then heat for another 20 seconds) or in a saucepan (bring it just to the boil).

4. Slowly pour the warm cream into the caramel, being careful not to burn yourself (the hot sugar will spit), then combine with a whisk. Once the cream is fully incorporated and the caramel is shiny, add the salt. Pour the caramel into a heatproof container and leave at room temperature.

5. Heat the oven to 170°C (325°F) and strain the apples to remove any excess liquid. Take your unbaked pie shell (see page 164) and fill it with a sixth (approximately 200 g/7 oz) of the apple filling, spreading it evenly across the base. Don't press it into the dough too much or it will affect your crust.

6. Drizzle the apple with about 3 tablespoons of caramel, then repeat with another sixth of the apples and another 3 tablespoons of caramel, followed by one more sixth of the apples; ensure the apple is evenly packed as you layer. Finish with 3 tablespoons more of caramel, with the option of drizzling over a bit more. (You'll be left with enough filling and caramel to make a second pie, or even a little more than that; see note.)

7. Lay a lid or the pastry ribbons you cut earlier (see page 164) on top of the filling in a lattice formation, then trim any excess pastry around the edge of the tart case. Brush any exposed pastry with beaten egg and sprinkle the whole top of the pie generously with raw sugar.

8. Bake the pie for 1 hour and 10 minutes. Remove from the oven and cool in the tin for approximately 1 hour. Remove the pie from the tin and cool on a wire rack for 10 minutes before serving.

Rhubarb pie

MAKES 2 x 18 CM (7 INCH) PIES

I've suggested making this pie with a lid, but there's no reason why you can't use the lattice pattern (see page 164) on top here. Likewise, you could make the apple pie (page 166) with a lid, if you prefer.

INGREDIENTS

970 g (2 lb 2 oz) rhubarb, leaves trimmed, cut into 2.5 cm (1 inch) pieces

270 g (9½ oz) raw sugar, plus extra for sprinkling

35 g (1¼ oz) cornflour (cornstarch)

3 g (¹⁄₁₆ oz) fine salt

1 quantity of khorasan pie dough, formed into a shell, with lid or strips (page 162)

1 egg, lightly beaten

1. Combine the rhubarb and raw sugar in a large mixing bowl, cover, and refrigerate overnight.

2. The next day, drain the liquid from the rhubarb into a saucepan, reserving ¼ cup (60 ml) in a separate bowl. Add the cornflour and salt to this reserved rhubarb liquid and mix with a spoon to create a slurry.

3. Place the saucepan over medium heat, stirring occasionally until the liquid warms to around 80°C (175°F), then stir in the cornflour slurry and return to a simmer, simmering gently until the mixture is clear and thickened.

4. Remove from the heat, add the rhubarb pieces and stir to coat, then cool to room temperature.

5. Heat the oven to 170°C (325°F). Add the cooled filling to the unbaked pie shell.

6. Place the circular lid on top, crimping the edge where the two pieces of pastry meet.

7. Brush the lid with the beaten egg, then sprinkle the whole top of the pie generously with raw sugar. Finally, cut a hole in the centre (approximately 1 cm/½ inch diameter) with a small, sharp knife to allow steam to escape while the pie bakes.

8. Bake for 50–60 minutes, then remove from the oven and allow to cool in the tin for approximately 1 hour. Remove from the tin, and cool on a wire cooling rack for a further 10 minutes before serving.

Chocolate and brown butter cookies

MAKES 20

We've taken the best parts of a chocolate-chip cookie and added a few twists that make them delicious for grown-ups, too, such as browned butter and khorasan flour (see page 232).

Khorasan is an ancient variety of wheat, meaning it hasn't been modified by commercial breeding. It brings a beautiful nutty and buttery flavour, which enhances the brown butter we use in this recipe. It's extremely gut-friendly, plus it bakes really well, too. My mother-in-law only uses khorasan for her cookies at home. Of course, if you can't find it, you can replace it with the same quantity of regular white flour for this recipe and you will still get good results.

Note that the texture of the browned butter is important. It's best to brown your butter the day before and leave it at room temperature so it doesn't solidify.

We prefer to slightly underbake our cookies then allow them to cool slowly to create that chewy texture.

INGREDIENTS

- 260 g (9¼ oz) unsalted butter
- 180 g (6½ oz) strong (baker's) flour
- 100 g (3½ oz) khorasan flour
- 1 teaspoon bicarbonate of soda (baking soda)
- 1 teaspoon fine sea salt
- 240 g (8½ oz) soft brown sugar
- 80 g (2¾ oz) caster (superfine) sugar
- 125 g (4½ oz) eggs (about 2½ eggs)
- 315 g (11¼ oz) high-quality dark chocolate (or a combination of milk and dark), roughly chopped
- Sea salt flakes, to serve

1. The day before baking, brown your butter. Melt the butter in a small saucepan and gently warm it, swirling it occasionally. Carefully skim the foam during the browning process so you can see what colour the butter is. Keep cooking until the butter is browned and smells nutty, then strain through a fine sieve into a heatproof container set on your kitchen scales. Weigh it to ensure you have 205 g (7¼ oz) of butter and discard any extra (or use it for another purpose). Set aside, covered, at room temperature, preferably overnight or at least until it's completely cooled.

2. The day you want to bake, place the baker's and khorasan flours in a large bowl with the bicarb soda and the salt and whisk to combine. Set aside.

3. Place the browned butter and the sugars in a stand mixer fitted with the paddle attachment and cream on medium speed for 2–4 minutes or until light and fluffy.

4. Switch to low speed and add the egg in two batches, scraping down the sides of the bowl and making sure the first batch is fully incorporated before adding the next. Mix until all the egg is incorporated.

5. Add the flour mixture, and mix on low speed for 2 minutes, or until it looks about 80 per cent incorporated.

6. Now add the chopped chocolate and mix until just combined.

7. Use a spoon or quarter-cup to scoop up pieces of the cookie dough approximately 60 g (2¼ oz) in weight. Roll each piece into a ball, then press to flatten into discs.

8. Place the discs on baking trays or in a proofing tray lined with baking paper and cover with a tea towel or a lid, then refrigerate for 4 hours or overnight to rest.

9. When you're ready to bake, heat oven to 185°C (375°F) and take the cookies out of the fridge to come to room temperature for 30 minutes.

10. Bake the cookies on lined baking trays, about 5 cm (2 inches) apart, for approximately 10 minutes until golden brown but still soft in the centre.

11. Remove the tray from the oven and leave the cookies to cool on the trays for 10 minutes before transferring them to a wire rack to cool completely. Once cooled, sprinkle with sea salt flakes.

12. Cookies will keep in a sealed container at room temperature for 3–4 days.

Pistachio, white chocolate and cherry cookies

MAKES 20

We love the pistachios that we get from Eric Wright at Go Just Nuts, grown on a farm in sunny Mildura, hundreds of kilometres north of Melbourne. He brines his pistachios so they're super crunchy. These cookies show them off fabulously.

INGREDIENTS

220 g (7¾ oz) plain (all-purpose) flour

80 g (2¾ oz) rye flour

5 g (⅛ oz) baking powder

8 g (¼ oz) bicarbonate of soda (baking soda)

8 g (¼ oz) fine salt

135 g (4¾ oz) unsalted butter, at room temperature

105 g (3¾ oz) pistachio paste (see note)

265 g (9½ oz) soft brown sugar

65 g (2½ oz) caster (superfine) sugar

65 g (2½ oz) eggs (about 1½)

40 g (1½ oz) egg yolks (from about 2½ eggs)

95 g (3¼ oz) white chocolate, roughly chopped

95 g (3¼ oz) dried cherries, roughly chopped

195 g (7 oz) shelled unsalted pistachio nuts, roughly chopped

NOTE

Pistachio paste should be 100 per cent pure pistachio butter. Read the ingredients list carefully. It can be bought from health food shops or specialist baking shops.

1. Place the flours, baking powder, bicarbonate of soda and salt into a large bowl and combine with a whisk. Set aside.

2. Place the butter, pistachio paste, brown sugar and caster sugar in the bowl of a stand mixer fitted with the paddle attachment. Cream the ingredients on medium speed for 5 minutes until light and fluffy.

3. Switch to low speed and add the whole eggs and yolks in two batches, scraping down the sides of the bowl and making sure the first batch is fully incorporated before adding the next. Mix until all the egg is incorporated.

4. Add the bowl of dry ingredients and mix on low speed until just combined.

5. Add the white chocolate, cherries and 95 g (3¼ oz) of the pistachios and mix briefly until evenly distributed.

6. Use a spoon or quarter-cup to scoop out pieces of the cookie dough approximately 60 g (2¼ oz) in weight. Roll each piece into a ball, then press to flatten into discs.

7. Place the discs on baking trays or in a proofing tray lined with baking paper and cover with a tea towel or a lid, then refrigerate for 4 hours or overnight to rest.

8. Half an hour before baking, heat the oven to 180°C (350°F) and spread the remaining 100 g (3½ oz) of chopped pistachios onto a plate or baking sheet.

9. Remove the cookies from the fridge 10 minutes before baking. Press one side of each cookie into the chopped pistachios, then place the cookies onto a baking tray lined with baking paper (you may need a few trays) about 5 cm (2 inches) apart, with the nuts facing up.

10. Bake for 7 minutes, at which point remove the trays from the oven and gently tap them on a bench before placing them back in the oven for a final 3 minutes or so until the cookies are browned around the edges. (The tapping will give you nice flat cookies with a chewy texture.)

11. Remove the cookies from the oven and allow them to cool on the trays for 10 minutes before transferring to a wire rack to cool completely.

12. Cookies will keep in a sealed container at room temperature for 3–4 days.

Chocolate sourdough cookies

MAKES 20

This is a clever way to use up sourdough starter that won't feel like a chore, believe me. Once you taste the subtle tang and complexity that your starter adds, you'll be looking for ways to sneak it into other sweets.

INGREDIENTS

160 g (5¾ oz) unsalted butter
250 g (9 oz) strong (baker's) flour
¾ teaspoon baking powder
1 teaspoon bicarbonate of soda (baking soda)
½ teaspoon fine sea salt
140 g (5 oz) caster (superfine) sugar
140 g (5 oz) soft brown sugar
15 g (½ oz) molasses
20 g (¾ oz) eggs (about half an egg)
20 g (¾ oz) yolks (from about 1 egg)
160 g (5¾ oz) sourdough starter (see page 36)
330 g (11¾ oz) high-quality dark chocolate (or a combination of milk and dark), roughly chopped
Sea salt flakes, to serve

1. The day before baking, brown your butter. Melt the butter in a small saucepan and gently warm it, swirling it occasionally. Carefully skim the foam during the browning process so you can see what colour the butter is. Keep cooking until the butter is browned and smells nutty, then strain through a fine sieve into a heatproof container set on your kitchen scales. Weigh it to ensure you have 120 g (4¼ oz) of butter and discard any extra (or use it for another purpose). Set aside, covered, at room temperature, preferably overnight or at least until it's completely cooled.

2. The day you want to bake, place the flour, baking powder, bicarbonate of soda and salt in a large bowl and whisk to combine. Set aside.

3. Place the browned butter, sugars and molasses in a stand mixer fitted with the paddle attachment and beat on medium speed for 4–5 minutes or until light and creamy.

4. Add the eggs and egg yolks and mix on low speed until fully incorporated.

5. Add the starter and mix on low speed for a few minutes or until thoroughly combined and smooth. It should look like a thick cake batter.

6. Add the dry ingredients, except the chocolate, and mix on low speed for 2–3 minutes until everything comes together as a dough.

7. Now add the chopped chocolate and mix until just combined.

8. Use a spoon or quarter-cup to scoop out pieces of the cookie dough approximately 60 g (2¼ oz) in weight. Roll each piece into a ball, then press to flatten into discs about 1 cm (½ inch) thick.

9. Place the discs on baking trays or in a proofing tray lined with baking paper and cover with a tea towel or a lid, then refrigerate for 4 hours or overnight to proof.

10. Half an hour before baking, heat the oven to 185°C (375°F). You'll bake these cookies cold, straight from the fridge, so once the oven is hot, place the lined trays in the oven and bake the cookies for 11 minutes or until golden but still soft in the centre.

11. Remove the cookies from the oven and allow them to cool on the trays for 10 minutes before transferring them to a wire rack to cool completely. Once cooled, sprinkle with sea salt.

12. Cookies will keep in a sealed container at room temperature for 3–4 days.

Maximum Enjoyment

Getting the most out of your bread

Tapas

I never opened that tapas bar I dreamed of after exploring Spain with Mia, but I didn't lose my love of small, simple bites based around great bread. Different styles of

bread lend themselves to different flavours, which opens up a huge range of possibilities. These recipes are just a few of my favourite combinations that might spark your own

→ Laughing Cow and anchovy tapa → Pan con tomate
→ Garfish gribiche on rye → Gilda tapas → JP Twomey's
beef tartare, mustard and cucumber tartine → English
tapas (aka easy Welsh rarebit, or amazing cheese on toast)

178—191

tapas ideas. All are great to share with guests
or simply make for a solo lunch at home. Skewers
are fine, but if you ask me, the perfect Gilda vessel is
a piece of bread.

Laughing Cow
and anchovy tapa

MAKES 8

Yes, it's Laughing Cow cheese, but if you think you're too good for this tapa then the joke is on you. This is salty, sweet and creamy in all the right places, all in a deceptively simple mouthful.

INGREDIENTS

3–4 large slices
   (1 cm/½ inch thick)
   of day-old country
   loaf (page 46) or
   ciabatta (page 74)
1 garlic clove
8 wedges of Laughing
   Cow cheese
1 tin of Ortiz anchovies,
   drained
Smoked paprika flakes
   (we use Pons brand),
   to taste

Quick-pickled onions

100 g (3½ oz) caster
   (superfine) sugar
100 ml (3½ fl oz) sherry
   (or red wine) vinegar
1 tablespoon fine
   sea salt
1 red onion, halved and
   cut into thin crescents

1. First make your quick-pickled onions. Stir the sugar into the vinegar in a large plastic container until it dissolves. Add the sea salt and stir to dissolve. Finally, add the onions, cover, and leave at room temperature for 30 minutes to pickle.

2. Use a cookie cutter to cut out eight 6–8 cm (2½–3¼ inch) rounds from your bread slices. It's important that your bread is the right size so you get the perfect bread-to-topping ratio.

3. Slice the garlic clove in half and rub one side of each piece of bread with the cut side. Top each slice of bread with three-quarters of a wedge of Laughing Cow cheese, then use a small palette knife to schmear the cheese. You can use a whole wedge if you really love your cheese!

4. Top the cheese with a few curls of pickled onion followed by an anchovy, garnish with paprika flakes and serve immediately.

NOTE

This recipe makes approximately 1 cup (250 ml) of pickled onions, more than you need for this recipe. Store any excess in a sealed container in the fridge for up to 2 weeks.

Pan con tomate

MAKES 1

Spain's favourite bread snack – pan con tomate – is another one of those brilliantly simple dishes where attention to detail and quality of ingredients matters. It's no surprise that it's one of the Spanish tapas that really stayed with me after visiting. Adding ricotta salata is certainly not 'authentic', but it is amazing.

INGREDIENTS

1 ripe tomato, halved
1 slice of country loaf
    (page 46), sliced
    2 cm (¾ inch) thick
    (see note)
1 garlic clove, halved
Extra-virgin olive oil
    (the best quality
    you can find)
20 g (¾ oz) ricotta salata

1. Heat a cast-iron chargrill pan to medium-high. Meanwhile, grate each half of your tomato, starting with the flesh side, on a box grater that you've set over a plate. Keep going until you're pushing the skin right up against the box grater, but be careful with your fingers. Season the grated tomato with a little sea salt and freshly ground pepper.

2. Once the pan is hot, toast your bread on both sides to your liking. Allow to cool very briefly, then rub the cut sides of the garlic very generously over the bread. Spoon the tomato purée onto the bread, drizzle with olive oil, then grate the ricotta salata very generously over the top. Serve immediately.

NOTE

At home I like to chargrill this bread on a cast-iron grill as it is a little too thick to put in the toaster. Plus that char that you get on the bread adds to the flavour. But if you can fit it in your toaster, go for it.

Garfish gribiche on rye

MAKES 7–9 PIECES

JP Twomey is a chef who has been a long-time supporter of Baker Bleu, first when he worked at Andrew McConnell's restaurants and then at Carlton Wine Room. He was one of the first to ask for our dark rye, which he's used in some fantastic snacks over the years. Its complex flavours are great with oily, salty or sweet toppings.

This tapa is a great way to show off Spain and Portugal's incredible tradition of preserving seafood in tins. Garfish from Spain is in fact smaller than what we find in Australia. It's a less oily and assertive option than mackerel or sardines.

Lots of chefs have since followed in JP's footsteps, serving similar things on our rye. This tapa is a nod to JP and his impeccable taste.

INGREDIENTS

1 dark rye tin loaf (page 108), 2 days old, sliced 5 mm (¼ inch) thick
Sunflower oil (optional), for drizzling
1 tin good-quality garfish in oil, drained (we like the brand Conservas Emilia)
Smoked paprika flakes (optional; we use Pons brand), to serve

Quick gribiche

1 tablespoon chopped flat-leaf parsley
1 tablespoon chopped tarragon
1 tablespoon thinly sliced chives
2 teaspoons Dijon mustard
1 tablespoon chopped cornichons
1 tablespoon chardonnay vinegar
2 hard-boiled eggs, chopped
1 tablespoon finely chopped eschalots
2 tablespoons good-quality sunflower oil
100 g (3½ oz) whole-egg mayonnaise

1. Make the gribiche by mixing together all the ingredients with a wooden spoon. Season with salt and freshly ground pepper to taste.

2. You can choose to crisp your bread up in one of two ways: either shallow-fry it in a thin layer of sunflower oil in a hot pan for a couple of minutes and pat it dry with paper towel, or toast it. In either case, take care not to burn it, which can happen quite easily with this loaf.

3. Once the bread is toasted, add half a tablespoon of gribiche to each piece, schmearing it if you want. Place a single garfish fillet on top. Season with either cracked pepper or paprika flakes and serve immediately.

Gilda tapas

MAKES 8

A snack playing on the Gilda, the immensely popular Basque bar snack (and sure, call it a pintxo instead of a tapa) most often featuring an anchovy, a fat olive and a Guindilla pepper threaded onto a cocktail skewer. Skewers are fine, but undoubtedly the perfect vessel is a good piece of bread, especially with ingredients that pack such a powerful punch. Prepare yourself for a one-bite wonder.

INGREDIENTS

2 large slices (1 cm/
½ inch thick) of
day-old country loaf
(page 46) or ciabatta
(page 74)
1 garlic clove
1 jar olive tapenade
or olive jam (we like
Mount Zero)
8 pickled Guindilla
peppers
8 cornichons
1 tin Ortiz anchovy fillets
in oil, drained

1. Use a cookie cutter to cut out eight 4–5 cm (1½–2 inch) rounds from your bread slices. It's important that your bread is the right size so you get the perfect bread-to-topping ratio.

2. Slice the garlic clove in half and rub one side of each piece of bread with the cut side. Spread a teaspoon of olive tapenade on each piece, on the same side you rubbed with garlic.

3. Lay a Guindilla pepper and a cornichon on each piece of bread, then drape and fold an anchovy fillet over the top. Serve immediately.

These pack a powerful punch. Prepare yourself for a one-bite wonder.

JP Twomey's beef tartare, mustard and cucumber tartine

SERVES 1–2

'I've always loved an open sandwich, and when I tried Mike's rye and caraway loaf for the first time, I knew it would be perfect for a raw beef tartine. The bread's spices and ever-so-sweet flavours work great with the beef and mustard in this preparation. That said, you can also substitute some fish for the beef in the tartare. Tuna or snapper both work well.

'You will end up with extra mustard cream but it's a great thing to have in the fridge for other sandwiches, or I like to serve it with some sliced smoked ham, boiled potatoes and a hunk of fresh sourdough country loaf.'

INGREDIENTS

1 slice rye-caraway loaf (page 56)
3–4 thin slices of Lebanese (short) cucumber, cut with a knife or on a mandoline

Beef tartare

80 g (2¾ oz) good-quality beef (fillet, rump or sirloin work well), cut into 1 cm dice
½ spring onion (scallion), green part only, thinly sliced
½ teaspoon Worcestershire sauce
1 anchovy fillet (I like Ortiz), finely chopped
1 teaspoon olive oil

Mustard cream

35 g (1¼ oz) Dijon mustard
8 g (¼ oz) hot English mustard
30 g (1 oz) cornichons, finely chopped
¼ cup (60 ml) pure (single) cream

1. For the beef tartare, mix all ingredients in a bowl until well incorporated, then season to taste with salt and freshly ground pepper. Chill in the fridge until needed.

2. For the mustard cream, whisk the mustards together until smooth, then fold in the cornichons and cream. Chill in the fridge until needed.

3. To assemble, spoon the beef tartare onto the bread, then add 1 teaspoon of mustard cream on top. (Leftover mustard cream can be stored in an airtight container in the fridge for 4 to 5 days for another use; you can also freeze it.)

4. Finish with the cucumber slices, being sure to season them with some more salt and pepper. Cut it in half to serve two people.

English tapas (aka easy Welsh rarebit, or amazing cheese on toast)

SERVES 1

The British answer to tapas might just be Welsh rarebit. I've cut a few corners here, keeping in mind that the time I most feel like eating rarebit is when I've had a few drinks. It's so comforting, but there's no way I'm doing a roux, pulling out saucepans or waiting for things to cool. This is my shortcut. Enjoy it just before you hit the hay or as a light dinner to soak up you know what.

As essential as good bread is to this recipe, so is the grill setting of your oven. This allows you to toast the bread but also melt the cheese. If yours doesn't have this capability, you may not enjoy this sandwich at its fullest.

I recommend slicing your bread to about 2.5 cm (1 inch) thick to best soak up the oil and butter.

INGREDIENTS

2 slices rye-caraway (page 56) or country loaf (page 46), sliced to your desired thickness

30–40 g (1–1½ oz) unsalted butter, for spreading

1 teaspoon (or more depending on your taste) hot English or Dijon mustard

80–90 g (2¾–3¼ oz) aged cheddar (clothbound if possible), coarsely grated

Cayenne pepper, to taste

Worcestershire sauce, to taste

1. Heat your oven grill to high while you prepare your ingredients. You want them all ready to go once your bread is toasted.

2. Once the grill is piping hot, place your slices of bread on a pizza pan or tray (things will get messy later). Toast the bread, turning halfway, for 1–2 minutes until golden on both sides, then remove from the grill and butter very liberally. Keep the grill on.

3. Allow the butter to melt and sink into your toast, then liberally apply your mustard. Finally, add the cheese and return each slice of bread to the grill until the cheese has completely melted. You want it bubbly and blistered, so don't pull it out too soon, about 2–3 minutes.

4. Remove from the grill and allow to cool for 1 minute, then use a small paring knife to score the melted cheese in a large crisscross pattern. Dust the cheese with cayenne pepper, sprinkle with sea salt and black pepper, then douse liberally with Worcestershire sauce, which will soak in between the crisscrosses. Serve immediately.

Sandwiches

The sandwich is such a staple in Australia and other Western countries that it can often be thrown together without much care. How much effort can you put into something you eat every day? That's not how we see things. There's almost a science to making a great sandwich. It's something that opening our Sydney bakery with Neil has made us appreciate even more. He's a sandwich fanatic! We have two of his

192–209

recipes here, but he could have given us many, many more. Because we supply bread to so many other top sandwich makers, we asked a couple of them to contribute their favourite sandwiches, too.

Neil Perry's tuna salad sandwich

MAKES 4 SANDWICHES

'This is a very light and tasty sandwich, and it's not difficult. You just make a lovely tuna salad, throw in the lettuce for crunch and lay it all on some quality bread and butter. Of course, you could use a roll if you prefer. I've suggested a few other variations below.'

INGREDIENTS

8 slices seeded spelt loaf
(page 58)
Softened butter, as much
as you like (I love a lot)
2 baby gem lettuces,
pulled apart, leaves
washed and dried

Tuna salad

425 g (15 oz) canned
tuna in oil, drained
2 celery sticks,
finely diced
12 Gordal olives, pitted
and roughly chopped
80 g (2¾ oz) mayonnaise
3 flat-leaf parsley sprigs,
finely chopped
½ red onion, finely diced
½ dill pickle, finely diced

1. To make the tuna salad, flake the tuna into large pieces over a mixing bowl, then add all remaining ingredients and fold to combine. Taste and adjust the seasoning with sea salt and freshly ground white pepper as necessary.

2. Place the bread on a board and spread each slice evenly with butter. Divide the lettuce among four pieces of bread, then spoon a quarter of the tuna salad over each. Top with the remaining slices of bread to enclose the filling. Slice in half and serve immediately.

VARIATIONS

This sandwich is also fantastic on rye or white sourdough.

To the salad, you could add things like chopped up roasted tomatoes, or some diced cooked potato. Or if you took all the ingredients for a classic tuna Niçoise salad, diced them and folded them through the mayonnaise, that would be very tasty indeed.

These flavours would also be perfect with chopped king prawns or even some shredded roast chicken in place of tuna.

Ash McBean's steak and ricotta sandwich

MAKES 1 SANDWICH

Everyone loves a steak and cheese sandwich, but who says it has to be rich and heavy? This recipe from Ash McBean of Gary's Quality Meats is a surprising combination of zingy, fresh flavours that people often think sounds odd until they try it. The plum, chilli and basil add an incredible amount of flavour to the eye fillet, which is a cut that sometimes lacks a bit of oomph.

'The perfect occasion for this is on a hot day when you have a few people over,' says McBean. 'I find laying out all the ingredients in front of you and creating an assembly line works the best, plus your guests will think you're a real whiz in the kitchen!'

INGREDIENTS

200 g (7 oz) free-range
    eye fillet, at room
    temperature (see tip)
Neutral oil, for drizzling
2 slices country loaf
    (page 46), 2–2.5 cm
    (¾–1 inch) thick
100 g (3½ oz) ricotta
Plum jam, to taste
1 red birdseye chilli,
    seeds removed,
    thinly sliced
¼ red onion, thinly sliced
¼ bunch basil,
    leaves picked

1. Season the eye fillet all over with salt and freshly ground pepper. Heat a frying pan over medium-high heat, add a drizzle of oil, then add the steak and cook, flipping it halfway, to medium-rare. Depending on the fillet's thickness, this could take between 2 and 3 minutes for each side. Allow the fillet to rest for at least 5 minutes before slicing.

2. While you're waiting for your steak to rest, spread one slice of bread with a generous amount of ricotta, and the other with a generous amount of plum jam.

3. Thinly slice the steak and lay the slices evenly on top of the ricotta. Sprinkle the sliced chilli and the onion over the steak, then place 10–15 basil leaves over the chilli. Top it all with the slice of bread spread with plum jam. Slice and enjoy.

TIP

Take your steak out of the fridge at least an hour before cooking. When it is at room temperature, it cooks more evenly.

Return to Sydney

Whether you believe in fate or not, opening a bakery in the city where Mia and I grew up and doing it in partnership with the guy who started one of the first restaurants I worked in is pretty surreal.

One person called it early, though. When we first opened the bakery in 2016, my cousin said to me, 'This is going to go so well that you're going to come back to Sydney with this business.' He was a rarity among the people telling us we were crazy. In fact, we thought he was crazy. But reality is stranger than fiction.

The way our Sydney bakery came about was even like a fantasy. I got a phone call out of the blue in April 2020, when most of Australia was in lockdown due to coronavirus. It was Neil Perry, one of Australia's most famous chefs, calling to ask if we'd ever considered opening a bakery in Double Bay, a ritzy harbourside suburb of Sydney.

I told him he was crazy and didn't think anything more of it. The phone calls kept coming.

'How many square metres do you need? How much bread do you think you can bake?'

This continued throughout 2020 when Melbourne was sealed off from the rest of the world. Finally, we were able to travel to Sydney to meet with Neil and see the site he had in mind. He was opening a new restaurant and had long talked about somehow getting our bread up to Sydney. Having it baked next door was his latest bright idea.

Mia and I were both quite sure that nothing would come of it. We also had plenty else to keep us busy, including building a second bakery in Melbourne. Our architect for that project came with us to Sydney to give us her opinion on Neil's proposed site.

When she said, 'I think you have to do it', my reaction was, 'I don't want to hear that!' The whole trip, I was hoping someone would say or do the wrong thing and we'd just go home.

That night, the opposite happened. Neil took us to Rockpool Bar & Grill, which he founded but later sold, and set about wooing us without us even realising we were being wooed. Lots of the staff still knew him. Some of them were going to help him open his new restaurant. There was a rare energy and camaraderie still there after 20-plus years.

The effect was intoxicating. I remember sitting there, trying to make excuses about why we couldn't do another bakery, but I was also thinking: when has this happened to anyone?

Mia and I got back to our hotel room and asked each other, 'What just happened? Neil Perry wants to go into business with us?' Mia, being the anchor of the business, snapped out of it and put the brakes on. She wanted more documentation, meetings with our accountant, the nitty gritty sorted out. To his credit, Neil did everything we asked for.

Fast-forward two years and we have a gleaming bakery in Sydney, designed by the same architect who did our Hawksburn store in Melbourne, with splashes of Yves Klein blue everywhere.

It's a world away from building our own bakery in Caulfield just a few years ago. In fact, the most stressful thing was not being in Sydney and getting invoices for things that we didn't even know were needed – like acoustic testing. But opening a business is never easy.

And yet I keep asking, 'What about this suburb or this site?' Mia, on the other hand, would be quite happy to sit still for a while, I think.

| Croissant $14 | Sandwich $10 | $7 | $10 | Orange Juice $12 |
| Baker Bleu Golden Granola $17.5 | Baker Bleu Health Crackers $11.5 | Baker Bleu Tote Bag $22 | Online Orders - Next Day Pick Up | |

Anthony Femia's 'Rare Sunday Off' sandwich

MAKES 2 SANDWICHES

'On the very rare Sunday morning that I'm lucky to enjoy away from my cheese shop, Maker & Monger, I like to make myself the perfect sandwich. This is a flavour bomb that ticks all the boxes for sight, smell, texture and stimulation of every taste receptor. I know it sounds way over the top for such a simple thing, but when you take your first bite of this sandwich you'll know what I mean.

'We use Baker Bleu's dark rye bread with our Flaming Reuben sandwich at Maker & Monger. The rye's remarkable sweetness and nuttiness is the perfect foil for the rich Russian dressing and wagyu pastrami. There's a similar thing happening in this sandwich, too.'

INGREDIENTS

4 corn cobs
80 g (2 ¾ oz) softened salted butter
50 g (1 ¾ oz) Comté, grated
4 slices dark rye tin loaf, 1–1.5 cm (½–⅝ inch) thick
200 g (7 oz) wagyu brisket pastrami (see notes), sliced 2–3 mm (¹⁄₁₆–⅛ inch) thick
Espelette (or aleppo) pepper flakes, to taste
1 large garlic and dill pickle, sliced very thinly on a mandoline
150–200 g (5½–7 oz) Somerset clothbound cheddar (see notes), thinly sliced
1 Lebanese (short) cucumber, thinly sliced on a mandoline
Handful of watercress, washed and dried

Condiments (optional)

Smoked jalapeño sauce, to taste
Sweet chilli jam, to taste
Sriracha sauce, to taste

1. Heat the oven to 180°C (350°F).

2. With the coarse side of a box grater, carefully grate the corn cobs into a bowl.

3. Add the grated kernels and their juices to a small saucepan with 40 g (1½ oz) of butter, place over medium heat and cook, stirring constantly to keep it from sticking, for 5–10 minutes until a thickly bound texture. In the final minute, add the Comté and stir through to melt. Remove from the heat, season to taste with sea salt and black pepper and allow to cool briefly (don't let it get cold).

4. While the corn is cooling, spread each slice of bread on one side with the remaining butter and toast it in the oven for 5 minutes or until golden. This will help reduce the density of the bread.

5. With the wagyu pastrami, I like to caramelise the fat and add a charred meat flavour. If you have a domestic kitchen butane blowtorch, place the pastrami in a cast-iron pan and then torch it until caramelised. Alternatively, heat the flat plate of a barbecue to medium heat and cook the pastrami on both sides for 30 seconds.

6. Once the bread and pastrami are ready, spread the creamed corn on half the bread slices (buttered side up) to a thickness of about 1 cm (½ inch). Sprinkle a good amount of Espelette pepper on top, then follow it with a single layer of sliced pickle, followed by the pastrami, making sure to distribute all the ingredients evenly between the slices. Place the slices of cheddar on top of the warm pastrami, followed by some cucumber and a small amount of watercress. Place the second slice of rye on top with the buttered side on the inside and serve immediately, with one of the suggested condiments on the side if you like. Alternatively, skip the second slice of bread and serve it tartine style.

NOTES

Don't use block or industrial cheddar, as the flavour of proper English clothbound cheddar is crucial to this sandwich. Montgomery's, Keen's, Westcombe or Pitchfork are all good producers to seek out.

Wagyu pastrami has an incredible fat content but if you can't find it, substitute regular beef pastrami that is not too lean and has a visible marinade on the rind. For a pastrami substitute, use freshly sliced ham off the bone, but don't flame it or grill it.

Neil Perry's curried egg sandwich

MAKES 4 SANDWICHES

'It's pretty hard to beat the combination of eggs, mayonnaise and rye bread. I love these curried egg sandwiches at any time of day, but if you wish to make them for breakfast and would like something less full-flavoured in the morning, leave the curry powder out.'

INGREDIENTS

10 eggs

8 tablespoons Kewpie
mayonnaise

2 teaspoons Keen's curry
powder

8 slices very fresh
rye-caraway loaf
(page 56)

Softened butter,
as desired

Iceberg or baby cos
lettuce, as desired,
shredded finely

1. To boil the eggs, place them in salted boiling water for 8 minutes, then remove and run under cold water to cool. Crack the eggshells well and leave the eggs to soak in a bowl of water for 10 minutes before peeling; this makes them easier to peel. It's also easiest to start peeling from the bottom of the egg.

2. Add the peeled eggs, mayonnaise and curry powder to a bowl and mash together with a fork until evenly mixed but still slightly chunky. Season well with salt and freshly ground black pepper.

3. Lay the slices of bread on a chopping board and butter them evenly. Place equal amounts of the egg mix in the middle of four slices of bread, then spread the mix out evenly to cover the whole slice. Top with lettuce and the remaining pieces of bread, and serve immediately.

VARIATIONS

This filling is also great on a rustic baguette. To make it a little lighter, add some watercress as well as lettuce. To go in the other direction, it's not out of the realm of possibilities to add an assertive cheese like Gruyère or perhaps cheddar or provolone; lay a few slices on top of the egg mix, before you top with lettuce.

To make this vegan, a tasty hummus can replace the mayonnaise and you could use fried strips of eggplant (aubergine) or zucchini (courgette) instead of the egg, or perhaps roasted and marinated capsicum (pepper).

Whatever the route you choose, slice them into finger sandwiches for a fantastic canapé.

Eli Weinberger's Tunisian tuna sandwich

MAKES 4 SANDWICHES

One of our longest-standing employees, Eli Weinberger, is also one of the most memorable people you'll meet. He brings an incredible energy to anything he does – and that includes personal grooming and eating sandwiches (that's him on page 22).

He used to own a café in Bondi called Lyfe, where he served a version of this sandwich. Between making coffee, serving customers and everything else a café owner does, he would bark directions at customers on how to eat the sandwich.

Eli's theory is that if you don't flip it regularly, you'll end up with one soggy side, as well as missing out on evenly appreciating the condiments on each slice of bread. Two years ago, he made sandwiches for the whole Baker Bleu team and our lunch break was punctuated by him yelling 'Flip it! Flip it!'

I'm sure that he would want you to apply this advice to every sandwich you eat, not just this tuna sandwich layered with Middle Eastern flavours.

INGREDIENTS

1 potato (about 120 g/ 4¼ oz), peeled
2 free-range eggs
95 g (3¼ oz) tuna in oil, drained
12 Kalamata olives, pitted and halved
4 tablespoons good-quality mayonnaise
2 tablespoons harissa
8 slices country loaf (page 46), 2 cm (¾ inch) thick
2 dill pickles, thinly sliced
1 tablespoon finely chopped preserved lemon (remove the flesh beforehand)

1. Place the potatoes in a large saucepan, cover with cold water, and boil until soft but not mushy, around 20 minutes. Drain, allow to cool, then cut into 1 cm (½ inch) slices.

2. Meanwhile, to boil the eggs, place them in salted boiling water for 8 minutes, then remove and run under cold water too cool. Crack the eggshells well and leave them to soak in a bowl of water for 10 minutes before peeling; this makes them easier to peel. It's also easiest to start peeling from the bottom of the egg. Cut into 1 cm (½ inch) slices.

3. Drain the tuna, add it to a bowl, and crumble it into small pieces with a fork. Add the olives, half the mayonnaise and half the harissa, and mix it all together well.

4. Spread the remaining mayonnaise on half of the bread slices, then top with the tuna-olive mix. Arrange the sliced potato, egg, pickles and preserved lemon on top and season to taste with salt and freshly ground pepper.

5. Spread the remaining harissa on the remaining bread slices, then sandwich these slices on top of the tuna-olive mix. Flip it as you eat it, naturally.

Reviving Bread

Fresh bread is undoubtedly one of life's great joys, but there pretty much always comes a time when you've got an awkward final sixth of a loaf sitting in your cupboard, or the heels of the bread that no one wants to eat.

Running a bakery, you get pretty good at coming up with ways to use leftover bits and pieces of bread. We and our staff are often bringing stray loaves home, or the awkward end bits that get left after making sandwiches, which all need to be a pretty uniform size.

210—219

Mia actually says she prefers the texture of old bread, with the chewiness that develops after a couple of days. It forces you to slow down, appreciate every bite, enjoy the texture. It's great with soft foods, especially, whether that's croutons with a smooth soup, or oven-dried ficelle with soft cheese.

The main piece of advice I'll give you is not to let your bread get too old before you attempt to revive it. Day two or three is the best time to tackle these recipes. Any longer than that, and you'll risk a knife injury trying to slice a loaf.

Croutons and breadcrumbs

To get breadcrumbs, first you've got to make croutons. If you need croutons, this is a bonus for you since you can make both at once. If you don't, ignore the croutons and just take all the bread to the next stage: crumbs.

The big question is, will you use your bread with crusts on or off? Leaving the crust on gives your breadcrumbs a deeper flavour and colour, which is perfect for making things like pangrattato. But crusts off means your breadcrumbs have a much higher tolerance for heat – they won't get too dark. If you were going to crumb fish or make schnitzels, I would recommend removing the crusts.

INGREDIENTS

Old bread, at least 1 day old but no more than 5, sliced (crusts on or off, depending on your preference)

1. Heat the oven to 100°C (200°F). Cut the bread into squares, slightly larger than the size of a sugar cube. Scatter the bread pieces evenly on a baking tray, trying to keep them uncrowded so they don't sweat or struggle too much to crisp up. Bake until the bread has dried out but hasn't coloured, about 30 minutes. Allow to cool. Now you have croutons. If you want breadcrumbs, keep reading.

2. Let the croutons cool completely (if you don't, you'll get moisture in the food processor and therefore in your breadcrumbs). Place the croutons in a food processor – don't pack too many in, it's better to do this in batches than overcrowd things – and pulse until they reach your desired consistency; I like to go somewhere between a panko crumb and a grain of sand. If you have dried your crumbs properly before blending, they will keep for up to a month in an airtight container.

Bagel chips

MAKES 4 CUPS

Don't give up on your leftover bagels – these crunchy morsels might become your favourite dip companion once you try them. I prefer to leave the slices whole for maximum dipping surface area, but see what you like. You can always crumble them just a little after they've baked and cooled.

You will need a good, sharp breadknife for this recipe.

INGREDIENTS

2 day-old bagels
1 rosemary sprig,
   leaves torn
1 tablespoon sea
   salt flakes
1 tablespoon extra-virgin
   olive oil

1. Heat the oven to 110°C (225°F).

2. Slice each bagel in half (through the hole from above), then slice it into thin discs, approximately 2–5 mm ($\frac{1}{16}$–$\frac{1}{4}$ inch), or as close to this as you can. Try not to go over 1 cm ($\frac{1}{2}$ inch) thickness.

3. Spread the discs on a baking tray, sprinkle with rosemary and sea salt and drizzle with olive oil. Toss to coat liberally.

4. Bake for 10–12 minutes, remove from the oven and allow to cool. Bagel chips will keep at their best in an airtight container for 2–3 days.

Your leftover bagels might become your favourite dip companion.

Lilli's health crackers

MAKES APPROXIMATELY 40 CRACKERS

These crackers from Lilli Reed, our manager in Melbourne, have become a staple grocery item sold in our bakeries in Melbourne and Sydney. The idea came from all the excess seeds that fall off our seeded ficelles, bagels and loaves. We store the seeds collected from our bread crates, mix through fresh seeds, and add oats and other ingredients on hand at the bakery to make these delicious, healthy and moreish crackers. They make the perfect vehicle for cheese or avocado, and are a lighter replacement for bread.

INGREDIENTS

230 g (8 oz) multi-seed mix (page 222)
115 g (4 oz) pepitas (pumpkin seeds)
25 g (1 oz) chia seeds
35 g (1¼ oz) psyllium husk
170 g (6 oz) oats
530 g (1 lb 3 oz) filtered water, at 28°C (82°F)
50 g (1¾ oz) maple syrup
15 g (½ oz) olive oil

1. Mix all the dry ingredients together. Place the wet ingredients in a large bowl, mix well, then add the dry ingredients. Combine all the ingredients with your hands, making sure everything is really well incorporated. Cover and leave to rest for 2 hours in the fridge.

2. While the cracker mix is resting, prepare your baking paper. You'll need two pieces of baking paper per tray, cut to the same size as each tray. Brush each sheet with a thin layer of oil.

3. Heat the oven to 170°C (325°F). Remove the cracker mix from the fridge and weigh out 170 g (6 oz) portions, placing each on a sheet of baking paper. Cover with a second sheet of baking paper and roll out to a thickness of approximately 3 mm (⅛ inch). Peel off the top sheet of baking paper and slide the rolled cracker, still on its sheet of baking paper, onto a baking tray.

4. Use your dough scraper to score the cracker mix into your desired cracker size. We suggest scoring in half lengthways and then making four or five scores the other way. Repeat rolling and scoring until you've used all of the cracker mix.

5. Bake trays, in batches, for 15 minutes, then rotate them 180 degrees, reduce heat to 150°C (300°F), and bake for a further 30 minutes until crisp and dry. Repeat with remaining trays.

6. Remove crackers from oven, allow to cool, then divide into portions along the scoring marks.

Panzanella

SERVES 4 AS A SIDE

Panzanella could almost be called a baker's salad – it takes your hard work baking a beautiful rustic loaf and showcases it, even when the bread might be past its prime. This recipe is made extra summery with the addition of ripe nectarines. To showcase the jumble of colours and textures in this salad, it's best to use a big serving plate, rather than a deep bowl.

INGREDIENTS

4 slices day-old country loaf (page 46; or dark rye (page 108) for a little more excitement), 2 cm (¾ inch) thick
Olive oil, for drizzling
3 ripe heirloom tomatoes
3 ripe nectarines (optional; they need to be in peak season)
Pinch of pink salt
100 ml (3½ fl oz) extra-virgin olive oil (the highest quality you can afford)
⅓ cup (80 ml) white balsamic vinegar (alternatively, white wine vinegar)
1 tablespoon honey
1 bunch of basil, leaves picked
1 tin Ortiz anchovies

1. Heat a chargrill pan or an oven grill to high. Drizzle the bread liberally with olive oil and then grill it, turning once, for up to 1 minute a side until the bread is crisp but not burnt, with visible grill marks. Once it's cool enough to handle, break up each slice into bite-sized chunks over your serving plate.

2. Cut each tomato in half and place cut-side down on the chopping board, then cut the tomatoes into uneven segments (all the rough edges are going to accelerate the almalgamation of flavours). Scrape them, along with all their juices, onto the plate.

3. Halve the nectarines, remove the stones, then cut the fruit lengthways into wedges. Scrape them and their juices onto the serving plate, too, then sprinkle everything with the pink salt.

4. Combine the extra-virgin olive oil, vinegar and honey in the bowl of a food processor, add most of the basil leaves (reserve some for garnish), and blitz to make a dressing. Avoid making this more than an hour before serving, or the dressing can discolour.

5. Drizzle the dressing over the salad and gently toss it all with care and love so you don't squash your tomatoes and fruit. Finally, arrange the anchovies evenly over the salad, scatter with the remaining basil leaves and serve.

Pantry Recipes

These pages are your reference point for all those bits that add that little extra to pastries, pizza, sweet treats or your loaves of bread.

A lot of these are also just nice things to keep on hand to quickly boost dishes, from breakfast-time through to dinner. Things such as the seed mixes, for example.

220—225

Others, like the pastry cream and rosso sauce, are especially helpful recipes to have in your back pocket as a cook. You can refer back to them time and time again.

MULTI-SEED MIX

MAKES 700 G (1 LB 9 OZ)

INGREDIENTS

200 g (7 oz) unhulled sesame seeds
200 g (7 oz) linseeds
150 g (5½ oz) caraway seeds
100 g (3½ oz) poppyseeds
50 g (1¾ oz) sea salt flakes (we like to use Tasman)

This is our go-to when we want to introduce flavour to anything: pastry, bread, pizza, cheesy dishes or even salads. The list goes on.

The secret to the flavour of this mix might lie in the unhulled sesame seeds. Why hulled sesame seeds even exist is a mystery to Mia and me. Hulling removes flavour and fibre. Always seek out unhulled seeds.

1. Mix all the seeds and the salt flakes in a bowl with a wooden spoon. Store in an airtight container for several weeks. If you're using this in a salad or to top a soup, you can toast the mix in a hot pan for a few minutes before using.

SEEDED SPELT MIX

MAKES 400 G (14 OZ)

INGREDIENTS

100 g (3½ oz) unhulled sesame seeds
100 g (3½ oz) linseeds
100 g (3½ oz) pepitas (pumpkin seeds)
100 g (3½ oz) sunflower seeds
5 g (⅛ oz) sea salt flakes

This is another full-flavoured seed mix, which we sprinkle all over our spelt and dark rye loaves. You can also use it to garnish salads, both leafy salads or ones made with a grain. Or toss the mix through breadcrumbs (page 212) for a supremely flavourful schnitzel mix.

When I was baking full-time, I used to drink coconuts then sprinkle this mix into the coconut, scoop out the flesh and mix it with the seeds. That was my baker's breakfast.

1. Mix all the seeds and the salt flakes in a bowl with a wooden spoon. Store in an airtight container for several weeks. If you're using this in a salad or to top a soup, you can toast the mix in a hot pan for a few minutes before using.

Why hulled sesame seeds even exist is a mystery to Mia and me. Hulling removes flavour and fibre.

SPICY SEED MIX

MAKES 450 G (1 LB)

INGREDIENTS

100 g (3½ oz) unhulled sesame seeds
100 g (3½ oz) linseeds
100 g (3½ oz) pepitas (pumpkin seeds)
100 g (3½ oz) sunflower seeds
1 tablespoon Keen's curry powder
1 teaspoon smoked paprika
1 tablespoon dried chilli flakes
1 teaspoon sea salt flakes
2 teaspoons extra-virgin olive oil

An extension of our other two seed mixes, this one adds in heat and spice. Use it to brighten a wintry soup, add it to cheese on toast or pasta, or incorporate it into your savoury baking. It's also great on roasted vegetables or added to salads, such as a simple tomato and cucumber salad.

1. Toast each type of seed in batches in a hot, dry frying pan over medium heat for 5 minutes until golden and fragrant, before adding it to a large bowl.

2. Toast the curry powder, paprika and chilli flakes in the same pan for 1–2 minutes until fragrant, then add to the bowl.

3. Add salt and oil, then stir to combine. Keep in an airtight container for up to 2 weeks.

QUICK-PICKLED ONIONS

MAKES 150 G (5½ OZ)

INGREDIENTS

100 g (3½ oz) caster (superfine) sugar
100 ml (3½ fl oz) sherry (or red wine) vinegar
1 tablespoon fine sea salt
1 red onion, halved and cut into 1 cm (½ inch) crescents

There are few things I cook that aren't made better by a handful of pickled onions. Their acid and crunch will cut through a rich cheese toastie, a chicken-mayo baguette, or a fatty cut of meat, like lamb shoulder. Plus they can brighten up salads and vegetarian meals.

1. Stir the sugar into the vinegar in a large plastic container until it dissolves. Add the sea salt and stir to dissolve. Finally, add the onion, cover, and leave at room temperature for 30 minutes to pickle.

ROSSO SAUCE

MAKES 400 G (14 OZ)

INGREDIENTS

400 g (14 oz) tin best-quality whole peeled tomatoes
2 garlic cloves
5 g (⅛ oz) fine pink salt
1 tablespoon extra-virgin olive oil

This will be the basis of most pizzas you choose to make at home. Red pizzas seem to be far more common in Australia than those with a white base. Buy the absolute best-quality tinned tomatoes you can, and you'll taste the difference.

1. Place all ingredients in a 2 cup (500 ml) container for which you have a lid and blend with a stick blender until smooth. Store in the fridge for 3–5 days.

GARLIC CREAM

MAKES 2 CUPS (500 ML)

INGREDIENTS

2 garlic cloves
2 cups (500 ml) thick (double) cream
1 teaspoon extra-virgin olive oil
Pinch of fine pink salt

Simple, but effective, this gives you white pizza in a cinch, but can also be used for pasta bakes, cauliflower cheese when you can't be bothered making béchamel, creamed spinach... the list goes on.

1. Place all ingredients into a suitable-sized container for which you have a lid and blend with a stick blender until just combined. Do your best not to overmix this.

2. Label the container with today's date and store in the refrigerator for 3–5 days. If you have a squeezy bottle, you can also store it in this (labelled) for easier application when you're making pizza.

THREE-CHEESE MIX

MAKES 650 G (1 LB 7 OZ; ENOUGH FOR 10 PIZZAS)

INGREDIENTS

200 g (7 oz) parmesan
300 g (10½ oz) semi-hard mozzarella
  (scamorza; see note)
150 g (5½ oz) cheddar

This is a perfect balance between sharp, salty flavours and stringy, melting cheeses that will satisfy your pizza topping, cheese toastie or even pasta bake topping needs. Keep some in the fridge and you'll never be far from a great cheese pull.

1. Finely grate the parmesan and add it to a large bowl.

2. Coarsely grate the remaining cheeses on a box grater and combine with the parmesan, mixing well. Store in an airtight container in the fridge for no more than 5 days.

NOTE

Semi-hard mozzarella (or scamorza) is the firm, pale yellow variety that's usually sold vacuum-packed. You don't want the soft white balls sold in whey for this particular use.

MAPLE GLAZE

MAKES AS MUCH AS YOU LIKE

INGREDIENTS

2 parts maple syrup
1 part water

This is what gives our challah and brioche breads that glossy finish that crackles when you bite into it. There's no reason you couldn't use this to roast naturally sweet vegetables, like carrots or sweet potato, for a salad. Just be sure to use a layer of baking paper underneath to avoid ruining your baking tray.

1. Whisk the water and syrup together in a small bowl until combined. I recommend starting with 2 tablespoons of maple syrup and 1 tablespoon of water. You can always make more if you need it.

PASTRY CREAM

MAKES 570 G (1 LB 4 OZ)

INGREDIENTS

300 g (10½ oz) milk
20 g (¾ oz) vanilla bean paste
110 g (3¾ oz) raw sugar
60 g (2¼ oz) egg yolks (from approximately 3–4 eggs)
30 g (1 oz) plain (all-purpose) flour
50 g (1¾ oz) pure (single) cream

Pastry cream – or crème pâtissière – is one of the basic building blocks of desserts, especially French desserts. With a texture that's actually closer to thick custard, it can fill fruit tarts, éclairs, mille-feuille or even doughnuts.

Armed with this recipe (which we scent with vanilla), you can come up with your own fillings for our Danishes, swapping out the apples on page 144 for whatever fruit is in season. Or you can omit the vanilla for your own flavourings, such as orange zest, pistachio paste or chopped chocolate. A quick search of the internet will help you figure out when to add different flavourings to your crème pât.

1. Add the milk, vanilla bean paste and 100 g (3½ oz) of sugar to a saucepan and bring to the boil.

2. Meanwhile, add egg yolks, flour and remaining sugar to a bowl and mix to a smooth paste with a wooden spoon.

3. Strain a third of the boiling milk over the ingredients in the bowl and, working quickly, whisk for 2 minutes or until the mixture is homogeneous. Repeat with the remaining milk.

4. Return the mixture to the same saucepan and, whisking, bring it to the boil over low heat. Whisk for 2–3 minutes until it thickens.

5. Remove from the heat, pour in the cream, and blend with a stick blender until smooth.

6. Transfer to a bowl, cover the surface directly with plastic wrap to prevent a skin forming, and transfer to the fridge to cool for at least 2 hours or overnight.

Acknowledgements

How to begin thanking everyone who's helped us? The first thing to say is that I wouldn't be where I am without my wife Mia. She's given up almost everything to make our dream happen and she's essential to everything we do – thank you so much. To our families, who have all contributed in different ways, but particularly Mia's retired parents, who were able to do all the things that we just couldn't get done ourselves. We owe you a lot.

I also want to thank all the people who have helped us along the way – there are too many names to list. From tradespeople to growers and suppliers, we've always made sure that we've looked after everyone who comes through the bakery, because we believe being good to people comes back around in the end. At times, favours from friends over the years have ended up being what's enabled us to keep the bakery going.

To the food community in Melbourne, we've been blessed by your support – from those first encounters with true food icons, who have become long-lasting customers and supporters of the business, we are humbled by the support these people have contributed to our success.

Thank you to all our staff, past and present, who make working in a bakery so rewarding. For the past couple of years of busyness, the challenges of COVID and opening new stores, we couldn't have done it without our passionate team.

Thank you to Neil and Sam Perry, their family and the Margaret team. IF Architecture and our accountants and advisors – you're so important to what we do, we wouldn't survive without you.

Making this book has been a huge team effort. A huge thank-you to Jane Willson for seeing the idea and potential and motivating me to persist with the book. To the Murdoch Books team,

Megan Pigott and Justin Wolfers helped push me along the whole way, thank you.

Emma Breheny, thank you for the many conversations and doing such a great job of pretty much writing this book for me. I had doubts of how I could do it, just coming out of a pandemic and opening a new store, and you had the patience to bear with me. Andy Warren, thank you for pulling such a creative and fun book together. Thanks to David Matthews for the careful edits and making everything so easy to understand.

Thank you to our pastry chef Gad Assayag, who was immense in helping develop the recipes for the book and baking for the photoshoot. Thanks to Isabelle Caulfield who knocked the recipe testing out of the park – what a star. To Parker Blain, who takes such cool photographs effortlessly in any situation, and Karina Duncan, who stays so relaxed in the chaos and delivered such beautiful setups, thank you.

And to our customers, some of whom are now our friends. You are the heart and soul of the business and we're proud to be baking for you. We never dreamed that so many people would put their trust in us. I thank you from the bottom of my heart.

Suppliers

These are some of our favourite ingredient suppliers and outlets. See pages 28–31 for our overall approach to equipment and ingredients.

Butter
We primarily use St David Dairy butter. Coppertree and Gippsland Jersey are also quality brands that are widely available in Australia.

Chocolate
We use Hunted + Gathered chocolate, which you can find online or from specialty grocers.

Flour
We sell Wholegrain Milling Co.'s sustainable premium white heritage flour at our bakeries, and their products – including khorasan, emmer and spelt flours – are available at wholefood retailers and online. You can also find quality, ethically sourced flours at wholefood suppliers such as Source Bulk Foods and most health food shops, both in-store and online. Where possible, look for flours that are stoneground. Some supermarkets have Bob's Red Mill flours, which are imported but a good alternative.

Olives and Olive Oil
We use Mount Zero olives, and Mount Zero and Cobram Estate olive oils, which you can find at wholefood retailers and some supermarkets.

Salt
Murray River Salt is an excellent local choice for pink salt. You can find fine Himalayan pink salt at most health food stores and some supermarkets.

Seeds
Most health food stores have a variety of good-quality seeds, including unhulled sesame seeds (see page 222). Source Bulk Foods has a wide range of seeds, available throughout Australia and online. In Melbourne, Terra Madre and Wild Things are great.

Index

Baker Bleu

bread for sharing

Online order? Step inside!

Published in 2024 by Murdoch Books,
an imprint of Allen & Unwin

Murdoch Books Australia
Cammeraygal Country
83 Alexander Street
Crows Nest NSW 2065
Phone: +61 (0)2 8425 0100
murdochbooks.com.au
info@murdochbooks.com.au

Murdoch Books UK
Ormond House
26–27 Boswell Street
London WC1N 3JZ
Phone: +44 (0) 20 8785 5995
murdochbooks.co.uk
info@murdochbooks.co.uk

For corporate orders and custom publishing,
contact our business development team at
salesenquiries@murdochbooks.com.au

Publisher: Jane Willson
Editorial manager: Justin Wolfers
Design manager: Megan Pigott
Designer: Andy Warren
Editor: David Matthews
Writer: Emma Breheny
Photographer: Parker Blain
Illustrator: Mike Russell
Stylist: Karina Duncan
Pastry chef: Gad Assayag
Home economist: Isabelle Caulfield
Production director: Lou Playfair

ISBN 978 1 92261 661 6

A catalogue record for this
book is available from the
National Library of Australia

A catalogue record for this book is available from
the British Library

Colour reproduction by Splitting Image Colour Studio Pty Ltd,
Wantirna, Victoria

Printed by 1010 Printing International Limited, China

OVEN GUIDE: You may find cooking times vary depending on
the oven you are using. The recipes in this book were tested
using a fan-forced oven. For conventional ovens, as a general
rule, set the oven temperature to 15–20°C (25–35°F) higher
than indicated in the recipe.

IMPORTANT: Those who might be at risk from the effects
of salmonella poisoning (the elderly, pregnant women,
young children and those suffering from immune deficiency
diseases) should consult their doctor with any concerns about
eating raw eggs.

TABLESPOON MEASURES:
We have used 20 ml (4 teaspoon) tablespoon measures.
If you are using a 15 ml (3 teaspoon) tablespoon add an
extra teaspoon of the ingredient for each tablespoon
specified.

10 9 8 7 6 5 4 3 2 1

MIX
Paper | Supporting
responsible forestry
FSC® C016973

tapas